# Undone

"*Undone* is a brave book, a true work of mercy for women who long to find healing from old wounds and discover their deepest identity in Jesus. By honestly sharing their own intimate struggles as daughters, sisters, friends, wives, and mothers, Carrie Schuchts Daunt and her fellow storytellers have opened the door to new freedom for their sisters in Christ. Scars are inevitable in this life, but *Undone* is a bold and loving reminder that when the Son frees you, you will be free indeed."

**Colleen Carroll Campbell**
Author of *My Sisters the Saints*

"Carrie Schuchts Daunt has wrapped a personal healing retreat in the covers of this marvelous little book. The thread of authentic testimonies woven together with opportunities for deeper reflection, healing, and wholeness will profoundly touch the lives of women searching for the glorious truth of their feminine identities."

**Christopher West**
President of the Theology of the Body Institute

"In *Undone*, Carrie Schuchts Daunt gathers fifteen radically honest and moving stories of women who have joyfully discovered in the midst of their shame and brokenness the freedom God offers to them. Through Mary, their knotted hearts were 'undone' by God's saving love in Jesus, enabling them to embrace and live out their God-given identities as daughter, sister, bride, and mother. This powerful little book not only gives voice to many women who struggle silently but also provides a hopeful way forward for those who desire deeper freedom. The prayerful guided meditations offered at the end of each chapter help women give God permission to set them free to know the truth of their feminine dignity. I highly recommend this book!"

**Rev. Mathias Thelen**
President of Encounter Ministries
Pastor of St. Patrick Catholic Parish in Brighton, Michigan

"You will find yourself in one story or another or perhaps sprinkled throughout. It is your story, her story, my story, our story. It is the story of the children of God whom he continues to pursue and redeem in his love."

From the foreword by **Sr. Miriam James Heidland**
Catholic speaker and author of *Loved as I Am*

# Undone

## FREEING YOUR FEMININE HEART FROM THE KNOTS OF FEAR AND SHAME

## EDITED BY
## CARRIE SCHUCHTS DAUNT

AVE MARIA PRESS AVE Notre Dame, Indiana

Foreword © 2020 by Miriam James Heidland, S.O.L.T.

---

Founded in 1865, Ave Maria Press is a ministry of the United States Province of Holy Cross.

www.avemariapress.com

Paperback: ISBN-13 978-1-59471-969-1

E-book: ISBN-13 978-1-59471-970-7

Cover image © Jasmina007/Getty Images.

Cover and text design by Brianna Dombo.

Printed and bound in Canada.

*Library of Congress Cataloging-in-Publication Data is available.*

THE KNOT OF EVE'S DISOBEDIENCE
WAS UNTIED BY THE OBEDIENCE OF
MARY; WHAT THE VIRGIN EVE BOUND
BY HER UNBELIEF, THE VIRGIN MARY
LOOSENED BY HER FAITH.

—ST. IRENAEUS

# Contents

# Part I: Daughter

# Part II: Sister

# Part III: Bride

# Part IV: Mother

# Foreword

The human heart is a beautiful diamond replete with many facets. Some facets shine with brilliance and sparkle and delight to be held up to the light. Others are dark and hidden and shrink from radiance yet still hold the same potential. It is the same in each of our stories. Every human person has a story—a place from which they came, a path they are on, and a destination to which they are headed. The journey is filled with valleys, plains and hills, mountaintops, dense forests, and boggy swamps. The reason we love a good story is because we are all part of a good story. We are part of the best story ever—salvation history. Each one of us has a part to play in God's epic story of salvation and redemption. We each know the journey of longing and loss, triumph and tragedy, and the ultimate hope for a love and communion that lasts forever.

One of the biggest barriers that keeps us hiding in the dark and shrinking from admitting our brokenness is the feeling of shame and isolation. Perhaps each of us feels as though we are the only ones who struggle with what we do or feel the way we feel about it. We fear coming undone and allowing ourselves to be seen as we truly are. We fear rejection and abandonment and the risk that speaking the truth might seem. But when we encounter the open hearts of others who share their stories with courage and vulnerability, we realize the truth that we are not alone and that every heart has a share in the common narrative of joy and sorrow. In fact, it is only through the willingness to share in the vulnerable places that true communion is born. An open heart is a beautiful heart.

In the pages that follow, you will encounter these aspects in each sacred story. What follows is an honest and authentic telling of the facet of a heart. You will hear both the brilliance and the darkness, but more importantly, you will encounter a real person living a real life who is still on the journey toward wholeness, holiness, and healing. None of the women writing these stories (myself included!) is perfect or has life all figured out, but each woman has encountered communion in her brokenness and hope in her healing, and she shines with the light of Christ a little more each day.

Reading through these stories rent my heart and made me weep from deep places of empathy and resonance. They brought new light into my own journey and inspired me with fresh joy and hope. You will find yourself in one story or another or perhaps sprinkled throughout. It is your story, her story, my story, our story. It is the story of the children of God whom he continues to pursue and redeem in his love.

You matter. Your story matters. Your life matters. May you find hope and healing in the diamonds of these pages. And may you know that Jesus Christ, the Lord of all and the One who loves you, has been with you all along.

Sr. Miriam James Heidland, S.O.L.T.

# Acknowledgments

Thank you to my husband, Duane. You are my *favorite*. This project could not have happened without your love and never-ending encouragement. To my children—Anna, Drew, Ryan, Jack, Luke, Lily, Elle, and Will—thank you for sharing me and allowing me to embark on this mission. You have all been so patient with me along the way. I love you all more than you will ever know. To my dad, Bob Schuchts, who lavished me with the Father's love and taught me how to share my heart. To my mom, Margie, whose prayers from heaven shower me with the grace I needed each step of this process. To my sister, Kristen, whose love and friendship are Mom and Dad's greatest gift to me. I am deeply grateful to all the beautiful voices who contributed to this book. I pray your voices bring truth and healing to women everywhere. Thank you to the courageous women who met in rooms 308 and 201 and all of the Good Shepherd staff, especially my pastor for the last forty years, Fr. Michael Foley. Thank you especially to Kiera, my sweet friend, who first invited me on this journey to become undone. To Kristi McDonald, my editor, and all the staff at Ave Maria Press, thank you for believing in this message and taking a chance on this first-time author.

# *Introduction*

## CARRIE SCHUCHTS DAUNT

"Knots!" she exasperatedly cried, screwing up her tiny nose. Throwing her tangled, beaded necklace in my general direction, she groaned in resignation. "Mommy! I need *you* to fix it!" Brushing her honey-colored curls off her sweaty face, she sighed, "I just keep making it worser."

"Let me see what I can do," I offered, as I picked up the knotted necklace from the cluttered floor.

When I eventually placed the finished work in her outstretched hand, she delightedly squealed, "Oh, fank you, Mommy. You did it!"

As I tended to the overflowing pot on the stove and her curious baby brother, whose fat foot was lodged in the crevice of the couch, out of the corner of my eye I saw her contentedly patter down the hall, clutching her restored prize.

My *little* girl is pattering off to college this year. While she still brings me her tangled teenage treasures, it is rare that I can help her loosen them. There are very few things more heart-wrenching than looking into your child's teary eyes and having no clue how to help.

Mercifully, we have a mother who is always capable of untying the tangles in our troubled hearts. *Our Lady Undoer of Knots* is a title bestowed upon Mary because she is foremost a mama. With the fierceness of a mother's love and a complete openness to grace, she deeply desires our restoration. Working on behalf of her children, she loosens the knots in our broken lives where sin and shame have twisted our desires, making our hearts a tangled mess. These knots, originating from Eve's control and grasping, have been passed from one generation to the next. Not one of us is exempt. Every daughter, sister, wife, and mother has inherited the effects of Eve's deception by the evil one.

Our feminine nature didn't begin this way. The very name *Eve* means "mother of all the living" (Gn 3:20). Before the first woman became a mother, she was Adam's sister (in humanity) and bride, and the beloved daughter of the Father. From the beginning, her relationship with God and with Adam was blissful and free. Adam and Eve were "naked, yet they felt no shame" (Gn 2:25).

Without shame, the first couple experienced the grace of full communion. Like a hose without kinks, intimacy surged. They knew and accepted each other in the fullness of their identity as man and woman. While their sin was the source of the fracture, their shame kept them separated from God and each other. God did not cover them with loincloths. Adam did not cover Eve, nor did Eve cover Adam. They each covered themselves because of their shame (Gn 3:7).

## THE SHAME CYCLE

Like Eve, we often respond to our own sin and brokenness in relationship by hiding. Working hard to conceal and protect the undesirable parts of our story, we tend to take cover. Because relationships are hard and people are broken, our feminine experiences as daughters, sisters, brides, and mothers are often marred by pain, sin, and separation. Relationships are at the core of our security and wholeness, so when they are fragmented, parts of our identity are damaged and broken. Instead of feeling deeply connected to those we are in relationship with, we feel alone. In our isolation, we long for communion with others and the opportunity to feel known. Yet there is a pain-filled part of ourselves we do not want anyone to know.

To protect this wounded place, we fortify and separate it from the rest of ourselves, carving a boundary through the center of our heart. Standing guard outside of this fortress is the strategic expert, shame. Shame works as a detour, insidiously preventing us from discovering and acknowledging the true source of our ache and inhibiting us from being ourselves, simply by keeping us partially, if not wholly, concealed from others.

I have experienced this reality in many seasons of my life. When I was a young mother, with three children aged three and under, I longed for relationship and connection. My husband was working long hours learning the ropes of his new career in a new town. Lonely, I jumped at any prospect of friendship that came my way. However, nearly every time I visited the cleaner, well-decorated homes where other moms served healthier food and spoke incessantly about their perfect lives (and the marathons they ran in their spare time—when I couldn't even find time for a shower!), I would leave with my rowdy group of toddlers feeling more isolated and alone than before.

The record that played in my head was, *These women have it all together and you are a mess.* I truly believed, *I am the only mom who wrestles with the many demands of motherhood. I am the only mom who has so many children born so close together. I am the only one who does not seem to belong.* These isolating experiences reinforced the pain that I had endured as a young girl (more on this in my story later in this book). My *grown-up* response, to protect my aching heart, was to hide the real me. Believing the lie that I was alone in this shame, I coped by holding back my heart and pretending.

What does it look like to constantly pretend? It is inviting others only into the presentable rooms of our hearts, the places that are warm and well ordered, acting as though the rest of us is just as tidy. It is putting up a facade so others cannot see the pain hidden in our deep, interior spaces. It is deceiving others and ourselves with the lie that these rooms of our hearts, like the disordered closets in our homes, simply do not exist. The truth is we will never be intimate with an ideal. We were made to be real.

# THE BEAUTY OF VULNERABILITY

Authenticity is hard to find, but it does exist. By the grace of God, a handful of authentic women came into my life during this messy season. These women allowed me past the front rooms of their proverbial houses. They invited me deeper into their stories, sin, and pain. Their honesty, vulnerability, and transparency penetrated my own fortress of shame. The witness of these precious women offered me hope and invited me to acknowledge the pain and sin I had spent a lifetime trying to hide. I saw in each of them what Pope John Paul II coined the "feminine genius." In his apostolic letter *On the Dignity and Vocation of Women*, His Holiness wrote, "In Mary, Eve discovers the nature of the true dignity of woman, of feminine humanity. This discovery must continually reach the heart of every woman and shape her vocation and her life" (*Mulieris Dignitatem* 11). I realized Mary was shaping each of these daughters of Eve who were surrounding me in community.

With these insights and the prompting of a cherished friend, I helped form an intimate group of women who began to meet, pray, and reflect specifically on the identity of women. Many of us embraced a new understanding and appreciation of our complex feminine identities. While the world encouraged women to grasp and control, we were diving into the redeeming truth of Mary's *yes* and learning the beauty of surrender and the gift of her radical receptivity. Mary's refrain became our refrain: *fiat—let it be done.* The more we spoke and lived this reality, the more the knots in our lives came untied.

To say this was an easy season would be disingenuous. Each of us journeying together as close friends found that the process of untying the knots made us feel *undone.* As the walls came crashing down, the pain behind the shame came into view. The deep places of our identity were laid bare. We were awaiting a new season of redemption.

Incredibly, the Holy Spirit redeemed each of us in different yet profound ways. Each encounter was so intimate and unique. The only common thread in each story of restoration was a willingness, like Mary's, to *let it be done*. In embracing Mary's posture of surrender, we were not simply tossing her our tangled lives and asking her to make the hard things easier. We were asking that we might become more like her in every way. We were imploring her assistance in opening the closed and hardened places of our hearts that were tormented by fear, torn by isolation, overcome by control, and ravaged by pride. We were begging her to fly to our rescue with the feminine virtues of receptivity, trust, and humility. We were asking her to uncover our deepest identity in and through her authenticity.

## AN INVITATION

This precious time spent steeping in my true feminine identity stirred in me a deep desire to bring the gift of authenticity and freedom to other women. Surrounded by a sisterhood of Marian hearts, I now present women's conferences under the mantle of the John Paul II Healing Center. Undone: Freedom for the Feminine Heart is a weekend of hope, healing, and worship. Through this healing ministry, our team has had the privilege of witnessing the knots of fear and shame in the hearts of women beautifully undone.

The raw and real testimonies included in this book are *your* invitation to discover the nature of your true feminine identity. Through the authenticity of these testimonies, you are invited to encounter greater truth and freedom in the comfort of your own home.

The women who tell these stories have waded deeply into the redemptive reality of Mary's fiat. With openness and vulnerability, they tackle topics such as fear, purity, marriage, identity, divorce, pornography, adoption, infertility, loss, rejection, abortion, single life, motherhood, miscarriage, illness, virginity, betrayal, body image, and beauty. In sharing these stories, they wish to proclaim the truth revealed to their once-broken hearts. Authenticity is possible. Redemption is possible. Freedom is possible. Simply hand Mary your knots, embrace her surrender, and uncover your true feminine identity.

## MOVING THROUGH THIS BOOK

This book is divided into four parts based on the four feminine identities outlined in Pope John Paul II's 1995 *Letter to Women*. An excerpt of this letter is included after the introduction. Each part begins with a brief overview of a specific feminine identity and then offers several stories highlighting the season where this primary identity was tangled and eventually untied. Each story concludes with a scriptural or spiritual reflection and study questions.

Each part of the book ends with a specific prayer for inner healing in that precise identity stage. The prayer was developed by Bob Schuchts (my dad), founder of the John Paul II Healing Center, for the Undone women's conferences. The healing prayer is meditative in nature, inviting us into an experience of grace in which we join Mary in relationship to the Holy Family and the Holy Trinity (*CCC* 533). Never wounded by sin, our pure Mother teaches us how to live in the freedom and fullness of our feminine identity.

This book offers many opportunities to press in deeper to your own feminine identity. The journaling exercises and prayer experiences facilitate areas of your own healing. This book opens new paradigms of truth. It also offers you the perspective that you are not alone in your fear and shame. Appendix III will direct you to other valuable resources as you embark on your journey to living undone.

# EXCERPT FROM POPE JOHN PAUL II'S LETTER TO WOMEN

## (1995)

This word of thanks to the Lord for his mysterious plan regarding the vocation and mission of women in the world is at the same time a concrete and direct word of thanks to women, to every woman, for all that they represent in the life of humanity.

**Thank you, *women who are mothers!*** You have sheltered human beings within yourselves in a unique experience of joy and travail. This experience makes you become God's own smile upon the newborn child, the one who guides your child's first steps, who helps it to grow, and who is the anchor as the child makes its way along the journey of life.

**Thank you, *women who are wives!*** You irrevocably join your future to that of your husbands, in a relationship of mutual giving, at the service of love and life.

**Thank you, *women who are daughters and women who are sisters!*** Into the heart of the family, and then of all society, you bring the richness of your sensitivity, your intuitiveness, your generosity and fidelity.

# PART I

## Daughter

### BOB SCHUCHTS

Before you were conceived in your mother's womb, you became a beloved daughter of the Father. He chose you from the foundation of the world and willed your conception. The moment you were conceived, you also became a daughter of your mother and father.

By God's design, every daughter is meant to be delighted in, securely loved, blessed, affirmed, nurtured, taught, disciplined, and given direction in life. When loved well, we develop the capacity to trust, play, pray, receive, obey, learn, and emulate our role models. Did you receive these gifts of daughterhood as God intended? Probably in part but not in fullness.

Unlike God who loves perfectly, our parents love imperfectly. Although made in the image and likeness of God and thus capable of great love, they are also descendants of Adam and Eve and of the generations that preceded them. They too have experienced brokenness. They have their own knots.

In this part, Melissa, Mary, Dorothy, and Judy share their personal reflections on what it was like being a daughter. You will learn about their joys as well as the knots that hindered them from freely receiving their identity as beloved daughters. As you read their

1

stories, I encourage you to think about your own experience of being a daughter. At the end of this part, you will have an opportunity to bring to prayer all you have experienced as a daughter—as a way of receiving a deeper blessing and healing in your authentic identity as God's beloved daughter.

# Sweet Surrender

## MELISSA PEREZ

Surrender is a funny thing. What does it really mean, anyway? Webster's dictionary defines surrender as "giving oneself up into the power of another." By definition, it seems simple, or does it? In my journey, real surrender looked like trust—trust in the power you are giving yourself up to. Trust in God. My surrender became a childlike rest in the arms of my adoring heavenly Father.

I first became acquainted with my need for surrender in the winter of 2005, on the feast of the Immaculate Conception, when my second child, Joseph Mayer, was born. His birth was one of the bright spots of my life. It was a joy to welcome him home and introduce him to his darling big sister. We had been home from the hospital for only a couple of days when I received a life-changing phone call. The person on the other end of the line informed me that my perfect baby boy likely had a rare metabolic disorder—phenylketonuria (PKU). She requested that I take my son to a hospital two hours away for confirmatory tests. I was shocked. I remember thinking, *This must be a bad joke.*

I immediately launched into attack mode, demanding the person's name, number, and employer. Who was she to tell me this news? After I got off the phone, I remember holding my son and sobbing. I sobbed over the possibility of this scary diagnosis and sobbed with a dreaded feeling of helplessness. I was entering into unknown territory. My husband drove us to the hospital while I cried on the phone with my mother, lamenting, "Why him? Why us? Why me?" That question of *why me* continued to haunt me for the next several years.

As I learned more about our son's diagnosis, I spent the next several years *controlling* my surroundings. Educating myself about PKU became my full-time focus. The kitchen was my classroom. I learned that the treatment is life-long and requires a multipronged approach of restricting many foods (especially proteins), utilizing medical formulas and medically modified food, and keeping daily food journals and weekly blood spots. As simple as that may sound, I assure you it is not. Food was present at every event, every function, every celebration, every family gathering, every playdate, every road trip. If food was involved, I made it my sole mission to provide food that looked the same, smelled the same, and tasted the same as, if not better than, everyone else's food.

God created me to be fierce, bold, confident, street-smart, quick on my feet, articulate, and personable. However, having all those gifts made it easy to rely on myself. Unbeknownst to me, I was an expert in control. I had it all together. With tenacity, I had overcome many adversities. PKU was no different. I accepted the challenge and, with much willfulness, did *my* best to keep my son healthy.

A few background details about my life help explain where my tendency for control began and why I desperately needed the peace of surrender.

First of all, I am adopted. There isn't a day that I don't give thanks for my life. I was welcomed into a family with four other adopted children. As the youngest, I was adored by all my siblings. Our parents loved us deeply, giving me a feeling of security.

At a young age I was diagnosed with dyslexia, and so began my early battle to overcome adversities. With much effort, I finished high school and continued on to college. Prior to graduating from a Catholic college in North Carolina, I was recruited by a local NBC affiliate. There I launched a successful career in marketing and advertising.

At my ten-year high school reunion, I reconnected with my high school sweetheart and soon after married the only love of my life. Before long, I gave birth to our first child, a beautiful little girl. Because I was adopted, she was the first blood relative I have ever known. After arriving home from the hospital, I held my precious baby in my arms and wept. The overwhelming love I felt was mingled with grief. The connection I had with her was unlike anything I had ever felt before. My mother, who was present with me, gently asked if I was all right. Through tears I managed to respond, "She is the first relative I have ever known."

All the questions surrounding my origins that I had carried with me throughout my life broke to the surface when I spoke those words. Questions such as, "What did my biological mother look like? Did she have blonde hair like me? Were her eyes blue or green? Why did she give me up? Why me?" That last primal question was the background music of all my experiences.

Thankfully, the broken record of shame didn't drown out my desire for God. A few years later, with the news of our newborn son's metabolic disorder and exhausted from constantly battling for control, I found myself craving quiet moments to spend in contemplative prayer. This prayer, over many years, softened me. God very gently started to pull back the layers that would ultimately bring me to a place of surrender. These moments alone with God allowed me to grieve the pain of being given up for adoption—a pain I had unknowingly carried my whole life. I had never acknowledged this pain because I knew I had a blessed life, with remarkable parents. I spoke boldly about being *chosen*. *Chosen* to live. *Chosen* to be God's child. *Chosen* by a family who desired me. How can feeling chosen my whole life equate to adoption wounds? God knew. He gently reconciled my gratitude and my grief. I refer to this time in my life of silent prayer as God tilling the soil. He was preparing me for a crisis I would not survive without him. He was preparing me to realize how courageous and beautiful true surrender is.

In 2010, when we were getting ready for the joyous occasion of our daughter's first Holy Communion, the crisis happened. We had relatives coming into town. I had planned every detail of this celebration and anxiously awaited the twenty-five houseguests due to arrive on Friday afternoon. On Wednesday of that week, prompted by my doctor, I begrudgingly went to an ultrasound appointment to have a silly little lump at the bend of my elbow scanned. Knowing I had only two days to finish preparing for the weekend, I was eager to go about the rest of my day, shopping, cooking, and cleaning.

Shortly after arriving home from my appointment, I received a phone call from my doctor. She asked me if I was sitting down. She explained that the findings from the ultrasound were of grave concern, and she wanted me to return immediately for an MRI. She informed me that conferring radiologists believed it was one of three possible types of cancer. Before we finished the call, she grimly warned of "limb- and life-saving measures." What? No! This couldn't be happening. Life came to a screeching halt. My world was turned upside down. I was scared, and I had no idea how to fix it or control it.

Over the next twenty-four hours, I received several more tests. Soon I was on my way to the same hospital that treats my son, for an appointment with an orthopedic oncologist.

For the second time in my life, I was out of the driver's seat, a passenger in my own car, while my husband drove me to the teaching hospital in Gainesville, Florida. I sobbed the whole way. Feeling totally helpless, I lamented, "Why me?"

I promptly underwent more tests. A team of admittedly baffled doctors examined me. As the main oncologist prepared to leave the room, he informed us that there was a larger team meeting to discuss my case and that he would return within an hour. That was probably the longest hour of my life. God had me just where he wanted me. With no other alternative, out of complete desperation I cried out, "Why me? Why me? Please, Lord, don't let it be me!" My husband hugged me tightly as I sobbed and completely surrendered my whole self, my whole life, all my worries, and all my fears into the hands of God. I had nowhere else to go. No plan B. *I* could not fix this. There was no way I could control this. The only thing I could do was melt into a puddle of total surrender.

In that moment, a miraculous thing happened. While my husband was holding me, a song echoed in my head. As if I had earphones on, I could hear music that no one else could hear. I heard "Breath of Heaven." It was beautiful and surreal. The song brought me into a deep peace. It wasn't until later that I understood what I had experienced. It was Mary's presence.

After what seemed like a lifetime, the doctor returned. He looked at me and said, "I can't really explain this. I can't explain how or why this has happened, but I am 90 percent sure this is not lymphoma or any other type of cancer. I think it is an internal hemangioma instead. Nothing more than a cluster of blood vessels like a pink birthmark. Why has it just popped up? I don't know, nor can I explain. I will continue to watch it."

*I'm sorry, what? Can you please say that again and slowly? Not life-threatening? Is that what you said? Not cancer?* I don't remember anything the doctor said after that. I don't remember driving the two hours home or walking into a house full of family and friends. I don't remember anything about the weekend I had worked endlessly to plan. The only thing I remember is my daughter receiving Jesus' Body, Blood, soul, and divinity. The tears that fell from my eyes were tears of the deepest gratitude. My daughter, in her radiant white dress and her giant, open heart, received Jesus, and I was there to witness it. When I thought that day couldn't get any better, God had one more message for me. At the end of Mass, our priest mentioned that that particular Sunday was Divine Mercy Sunday. He explained that Jesus' mercy is never-ending—always present and available to all who wish to receive it. That was it! That was *it*! God had shown *me* mercy. It took my wholehearted surrender to see how merciful he truly was. This was the turning point in my life. This was the moment when I finally understood surrender.

God has given me many more opportunities to practice surrender. He has mercifully and patiently guided me into deeper places of healing. He has shown me my root wounds of abandonment and unforgiveness relating back to my adoption and how those wounds led me to a tendency to control. He revealed that while he has granted me many gifts, these gifts are for his glory and not mine. He has also immensely blessed my son's health. It has been a struggle at times not to fall back into my old habits of self-reliance, but through my continued surrender, the Father has healed my deepest wound and answered my inmost question, "Why me?" *Because he loves me.*

## Take a Moment

1. Pray with the following passage from St. Faustina's *Diary: Divine Mercy in My Soul*:

   I am Love and Mercy itself. There is no misery that could be a match for my Mercy, neither will misery exhaust it, because as it is being granted—it increases.

   a. Read the passage once and become familiar with the text.
   b. Slowly read the passage a second time.
   c. Very, very slowly read the passage a third time, paying attention to the words and phrases that rest in your heart. What is the Holy Spirit speaking to you through this passage?

2. Do you believe there is a misery in your life that is outside of the Father's mercy? If so, are you willing to bring this misery to the Father of mercy?

3. What does surrender look like to you? Is it something familiar or foreign? Pray into what the Father may be revealing to you as you reflect on this concept of holy surrender.

# Not That Girl

## MARY BIELSKI

I love the Broadway musical *Wicked*.[1] I have seen it no less than seven times. The soundtrack played on a running loop in my car's six-disc changer the entire first year of its release. I would assign myself parts, belt out the ballads, and awkwardly harmonize as I drove.

For those of you not familiar with this Tony Award–winning musical, I should explain. The magical story takes place in the Land of Oz years prior to Dorothy's arrival. At the center of the story is Elphaba, a fiery, smart, misunderstood girl of emerald-green skin who becomes the notorious Wicked Witch of the West. Her counterpart is Glinda, the beautiful, blonde, popular sweetheart who becomes the Good Witch of the South. This rich story speaks of friendship, betrayal, hope, disappointment, and true love. And I love it all.

This soundtrack is my healing journey set to music. The sad ballad "Not That Girl" was the mantra of the lie that formed a twisted, tangled knot around my feminine identity and gave lyrics to the lies I had grown to believe. I was *not that girl*.

I was not the pretty girl or the chosen girl. No one would ever truly come for me. Not this girl. And it was easy to explain why I was not that girl. Fundamentally, there was something wrong with me.

Elphaba was a gifted girl who saw herself as different. And to her, "different" meant "defective." I have spent a good portion of my life feeling defective. Her story was my story, too. I might not have been emerald green from birth, but I certainly felt disqualified, rejected, and shamed. I felt defective.

As a little girl, I was a tomboy. I didn't just like to climb trees and play sports. I asked for toy guns for Christmas and action figures for my birthday. I had an aversion to pink. I wasn't like the other girls, and I could feel the disappointment rising in me as I began to tell myself that whoever I was, was wrong.

I have an early memory of coming home from preschool and asking my mom if I could wear boys' underwear. This was a request I was excited to make. Amy's mom let her wear a pair of Transformer briefs to school, and I longed for a matching pair. As I shared my enthusiasm, my sister, who was sixteen at the time, interrupted with a gasp of disgust and a grimace of horror at my request. Her scrutiny shamed me. I felt my cheeks burn, and hot tears stung my eyes. Confused and ashamed, I internalized my regret at sharing with my family what delighted me. *What girl wants to wear boys' underwear?* I asked, slowly beginning to agree with the lie I had picked up—something is wrong with me, I am defective, *I am not that girl.*

And right there in the kitchen, as inconsequential as it may seem, the enemy tightened a knot in my feminine heart that had been forming for quite some time and would take many complicated years to unravel.

In addition to my boyish ways, I had a learning disability and struggled with ADHD. If that wasn't enough to set me apart, I was also extremely tall. I am now 5'11", but I was every bit of 5'10" in middle school. I stood a foot taller than all the boys in my class pictures. I looked like a giraffe poking its head out of the herd of zebras.

The adolescent boys pounced on my weakness. My obvious differences made me vulnerable at the watering hole. Every morning when I stepped onto the bus, the boys would grunt my name in a low masculine voice: M-AA-RR-Y. My female body didn't feel very feminine. I felt unsettled in my own skin. Shame was a significant part of my existence.

I was to learn about my feminine identity from my mother. It was from her that I was to receive my first identity blueprint.

My mom was forty-one when she had me. I was the youngest of five children spanning sixteen years. I was a latchkey kid with two working parents in a highly successful family. Maybe years of orchestrating a busy home did them in, but the bottom line was that I didn't have guardrails. In a dynamic family moving a million different directions at once, I felt overlooked. In addition, my mother's struggle with depression kept us distant. As highly as I regard my parents, as deeply as I love them, and as much as they sacrificed, I must honestly say that I felt emotionally orphaned as a child. So, I fended for myself.

In high school, I had an English teacher who had a profound influence on me. She was the first adult woman who really sought to know me. I poured out my heart in her weekly class journal assignments, and she became my support. I went to her office during my free time to discuss ideas around culture, feminism, life, and meaning. As my one and only role model, she began to form my understanding of what it meant to be a woman.

My senior year, this teacher came out as a lesbian. As I listened to the romantic details of her personal story, I wondered if perhaps I was bisexual. Was this the easy answer to my complicated relationship with my femininity? Would embracing this identity clarify for me why I was so very different from everyone else?

High school did little to increase my self-awareness. I entered college with a determination to sow my wild oats. Late nights and keg stands did nothing to free me from my sense of unworthiness and isolation. Struggling with crippling depression, I hid behind my résumé, my social media filter, and my clutched list of successes. But the sense of profound unworthiness became a crushing weight.

I think the Lord often uses desperation to showcase his work. After a year of seeking meaning at fraternity parties, I fell in love with Jesus and his Church thanks to a persistent Carmelite nun, a dedicated youth minister, and God's profound grace. I have not been the same since. Despite my conversion and understanding of the Lord's love, the lies I believed tied me down for another decade. I struggled with debilitating thoughts of worthlessness, self-condemnation, and crippling shame. I knew I needed help. I knew I needed healing. At just the right time, a trinity of men came into my life in the most tender of ways.

Bob Schuchts with the John Paul II Healing Center[2]; Christopher West, best known for his courses at the Theology of the Body Institute[3]; and Fr. Mark Toups, gifted in his knowledge of inner healing prayer, all ministered to my heart in the kindest, most unexpected ways.

We can hide from our lies, but they eventually come to find us. Mine tiptoed in during a theology of the body course with Christopher West. When West began to unpack the story of Adam and Eve and the original wounds, something was triggered. I got pissed. A slow, snippy anger ensued in my heart, and I remember the Lord bringing my attention to it. Like a scab hardened over the wound, my anger was protecting me from my pain. God was gently revealing the central lie of my feminine identity. I resented any traditional view of femininity. I wasn't sure I fit in the box of femininity.

Soon after recognizing a tension within my feminine identity and the self-condemnation that accompanied it, I hungered for wholeness. My restoration came through Mary, our Mother. Near the end of a long retreat week of intense study, introspection, and prayer, Dr. Bob un-mic-ed himself to read the powerful proclamation of Christ's mission for healing. Reciting Isaiah 61, Dr. Bob thundered over us, God's people, "The spirit of the Lord God is upon me!" It loosened something locked in me. The Lord was present. The sounds of weeping all around me were proof. We were experiencing a Pentecostal moment beyond our ability to comprehend, a presence that surpassed understanding. Dr. Bob stopped teaching and moved to prayer, and I found myself in front of a large tapestry of Our Lady of Guadalupe. I allowed our Mother to nurture me with maternal affection as I remembered my loneliness as a child. She swung my legs across her lap and stroked my hair, whispering gently in my ear, "It's going to be okay."

My encounter with Mary's love melted me. It was in a specific prayer time, working with Fr. Mark, that I was led back to the memory of me as a little girl wanting to wear boys' underwear. Jesus came, and with him, Mary. Without accusation or disgust but with celebration and joy in sharing my adventure, Mary opened my feminine heart. The powerful moments of that prayer time completely healed that memory. I walked out floating and have not had an ounce of shame around that experience since.

Mary loved me with a love that pointed directly to the *wonderful* power of Christ.

All in all, I let the Father love me. He gently touched the edges of every wound, no ripping necessary. I know I am still not finished; I will never be finished. But I finally learned with my heart, not just my head, that I didn't need to be fixed in order for him to love me. God's desire wasn't to fix me. God's desire was communion with me. My only job was to show up as a child to be loved and let him love me.

While I still enjoy football and proudly own a drill, I love being a woman! My relationship with my mom has been restored, together with my identity as daughter. And, amazingly, I feel like I am a mother to the thousands of youth I minister to. I give talks about the theology of the body,[4] and I feel part of my mission is to help other girls, like me, who don't feel like they fit neatly in any tidy box.

St. Thérèse of Lisieux spoke about each of us as a precious part of a large garden. There are the elegant lilies, the simple daisies, and the fragrant violets, and the roses in all their splendor.[5] We all have different personalities, different gifts, and different callings. Every one of us has a place in the kingdom. We are all irreplaceable. We are all beloved. As we rise to know our identity, the world becomes a more beautiful place.

## Take a Moment

1.  Pray with the following quotation from St. Thérèse of Lisieux:

    > I understood that every flower created by Him is beautiful, that the brilliance of the rose and the whiteness of the lily do not lessen the perfume of the violet or the sweet simplicity of the daisy. I understood that if all the lowly flowers wished to be roses, nature would no longer be enameled with lovely hues. And so it is in the world of souls, Our Lord's living garden.

    a.  Read the quote once and become familiar with the text.
    b.  Slowly read the passage a second time.
    c.  Very, very slowly read the passage a third time, paying attention to the words and phrases that rest in your heart. What is God speaking to you through this passage?
2.  Which flower best represents you? Why?
3.  Do you believe the Father sees your unique beauty? Why or why not?

# The Weight of His Glory

## DOROTHY DERZYPOLSKI WAGNER

In some way, shape, or form, I have been on a diet for half of my life. As a girl, I never considered my weight. I was happy just being *me*. I loved to dance. I grew up confidently moving across a stage. I was confident because I knew my father's love. He was a caring dad. We would go watch airplanes take off at the airport, and spend hours outside telling stories and watching the stars. When my parents went through a painful divorce during my second-grade year, he quite literally bought me a pony. I was the apple of his eye. My two older brothers and older sister knew it. I knew it. My mom knew it.

My mom was also a loving mother. She knew and shared my love of dance. She took me to ballet, horseback riding, and debate competitions. We watched movies, went out for dinner, and spent long summer days together at my grandmother's beach house. She taught me to pray with the Holy Spirit and showed me what it meant to care for others and serve them in their time of need.

My mom delighted in me. My dad delighted in me. But they did not much delight in each other. Their story is another story, but it is also the beginning of mine. It is enough to say that despite their difficulties, their love buoyed me as a young girl.

When my parents separated, no one explained to me what was happening. I just knew my mom had left and my dad was terribly sad. Even when my parents reunited a couple years later, something seemed awry. My dad would drink at night and a sadness would envelop him. At the time, I did not understand he was suffering from post-traumatic stress disorder after his service in Vietnam.

The enemy sowed lies, like weeds, in my heart to attack my self-esteem. Lies that for many years I heard but did not believe. On the playground in third grade, a group of girls made fun of my weight and my clothes during a dress-down day at our private Catholic school. Another time, I was the only girl not invited to a birthday party at the beach. A well-intended uncle once told me that "a couple of laps around the track would really help you be a better dancer." A big brother tried to encourage me by saying that I had "a gorgeous smile" and when I grew "taller and thinner," I "could be a model." I knew everyone was always discussing diets. In nutrition class, I learned about calories. A "helpful" coach gave me a crash course in calorie control and protein to assist me in "leaning out and building muscle" because he saw so much potential in me. All of these moments were scattered seeds that never took root because my dad's love immediately cut them down. I walked in the confidence of my father's love for me. Through that, I found a relationship with my Father in heaven.

Toward the end of my sophomore year of high school, something changed. I watched my father crumble under the weight of alcoholism and post-traumatic stress disorder. Coming home one day after a swim meet, I found him in a terrible state. He divulged that he should have died in Vietnam and that he wished now that he was not alive. In that moment, I did not understand the horrors he had experienced or the heroic choices he had made. I only knew my rock, my hero, my dad sitting before me, wished he was dead. My response in that moment was to plead with him. I argued that if he had died, I would not exist.

Although I was fourteen years old, this moment stands in time immortal for me. Like a little girl twirling in an Easter dress, saying, "Look at me, Daddy, am I lovely?" I truly thought that my presence and beauty would bring him back to joy. Not this time. Instead, he just looked at me with his red, puffy eyes and with a sad, slow slur said, "That doesn't matter." My buoy sank like a lead weight to the depths of the sea. I felt completely out of control. I could not help him. I could not bring him happiness in his pain. Then a cunning voice whispered the lie: *You never have been lovely enough.*

Agreeing with that lie caused the rest of the lies spoken over me to take root. Somehow, in that moment and the difficult months that followed, I accepted that this was entirely my fault. I should have been able to make my dad happy. I should have been able to make my mom happy. I should have been able to make them happy together. At that time, it was well beyond my understanding that the Lord was bringing about a mighty healing in my father's life and in my parents' relationship. In the midst of that time of trial, I did not know that someday they would be deeply in love again, celebrating fifty years of marriage and eighteen years of my dad's sobriety. I only knew that my teenage-self felt out of control and out of familiar territory. My parents sent me to live with my grandmother, five hours away, while they worked out some of the most difficult days of their lives.

It was during this time that I became aware of every imperfection. All those weeds planted over the years were furiously sprouting because my father wasn't there to cut them down. I began to restrict my diet to less than six hundred calories a day. In addition to swimming four to five hours daily, I was also striving for absolute academic perfection.

I carried this obsession with self-control and perfectionism with me to college. While I was outwardly confident and was well liked, inside I was holding on as tight as I could with clenched fists. I was afraid to let anything slip away. I believed that I was not enough. Suddenly every lie was my truth: *I did need to lean up, be taller, thin out, take a couple laps around the track* . . .

Somewhere in those years, I was introduced to a dark idea I saw in a popular movie about dancing. I could make myself get sick after eating. And so it began. The first time I snuck away was on my sixteenth birthday. I was celebrating at a Mexican restaurant with my friends. I had certainly consumed more than my six-hundred-calorie limit. So I slipped away to the restroom, flipped up the toilet lid, and made myself sick. I remember thinking, *What the hell is wrong with me?* Afterward the shame was mingled with a strange satisfaction. I could control my weight. I soon became an expert at "slipping away."

When I was twenty, I went on a retreat with a Catholic campus ministry and made a conscious choice to stop my bulimic tendencies. I confessed everything. However, within a week I found myself kneeling over the bathroom toilet again. Curled up on the floor weeping, I begged the Lord to help me to stop. I wanted so badly to be free. This was the first time I pleaded with my heavenly Father to take this thorn from my side.

The Lord did not reach down that day and heal me of my self-criticism, my obsession with control, or my fear of imperfection. Instead, on that particular day, he made me aware that I needed him. I really, truly *needed* him. Thankfully, counseling, prayer, and friends who held me accountable helped me to be in a good place by the time I walked down the aisle at twenty-two years old and married my husband, Nicholas. Although I was fit and lean on that day, I still wasn't content with my weight. I could never look at myself and find beauty. However, my husband did. He lavished his loving gaze upon me, and that was a healing salve. I found peace from my "thorn" for a while by eating a restrictive diet, running three miles a day, and embracing my husband's affection.

Soon, however, I found myself spiraling again. In our second year of marriage, Nicholas and I celebrated the birth of our son, and then thirteen months later the birth of our daughter. Two pregnancies brought thirty ticks up the scale, interiorly wrecking me. I no longer had the lean body of a college swimmer and runner. No, I was flabby and plump. I was ashamed of my weight, and I was ashamed to be ashamed because, *really, what kind of wife and mother still struggles with this stuff?* About that time, my husband and I hit the rocky years of our marriage. Parenthood stretched us, and we fought about everything from family planning to meals to scheduling to whether or not to stir the pasta sauce with the meatball spoon. Suddenly my husband's gaze was not always affectionate and loving. I began to feel out of control, and I hated my imperfections. Sheepishly I began to take my bulimia and self-criticism to Confession again. I felt such shame being a young wife and mother with two beautiful children who was still struggling like a teenager with feeling fat. Good and holy priests in the confessional would speak kind words about the beauty of motherhood and femininity, and I would shrug it off, sure that if I could just shed thirty pounds I would be okay.

Pregnant with my third child, I went on a women's retreat in the mountains. On a long walk around a lake with a fierce and holy priest, I confessed my self-criticism, my shame, my bulimia, my need to control, and my perfectionism. With great humility, he asked me if I idolized my husband's approval, and I confessed that I found myself desperate for Nicholas's support and affection. This priest asked me if I rested in the loving gaze of the heavenly Bridegroom. I knew I did not. Concluding that grace-filled Confession, I went to sit with our Lord and pray. It was then that he brought me back to that living room after the swim meet during my sophomore year of high school. I saw my dad, whom I idolized, broken and weak, and relived him telling me that he wished he was dead. I saw myself pleading with him to see me and rejoice in me, and I felt the resonating sting of rejection and insufficiency. I saw in my heart of hearts my world crumbling and felt the total fear of being out of control. *Yet something was different.* Someone was standing there just beyond my dad. *I saw the Lord* and he looked at me with a deep gaze of love. Tears rolled down his face. I felt the ache of his heart, as though I was on a boat tossed in a storm and he was longing to still the waters for me. In his loving gaze, I encountered so much mercy and compassion and the invitation to grace. This time, instead of hiding the fear, shame, and sense of powerlessness I was experiencing, I cried out to Jesus. A second time I asked him to remove this thorn. He answered *me*! In that moment, I knew I would never make myself sick again.

My third and fourth children were born, and I grew as a wife, mother, and woman of God. However, I was still a sucker for every fad diet book, exercise program, and gym membership. Eventually I worked my way back down to my wedding weight through healthy eating and exercise. When I slipped on my wedding dress a couple months after our tenth wedding anniversary, I felt sure that I would look in the mirror and find peace and confidence. But as I stood there, I was painfully aware of my imperfections. A voice spoke from within me again: *You are not lovely. Change this . . . and this . . . and this . . . and then you will be lovely.* There I was, thirty-two, with four glorious children, speaking to myself as if I was thirteen years old. *When, Lord, will this stop?*

It was then that the mother of a good friend passed away. At her funeral on a Saturday afternoon, I watched her body carried into the church as the congregation sang the same song of worship that my husband and I had chosen for our wedding day. Overcome with emotion, I wept with a desire to live a life so wholly sold out for our Lord that someday I would stand like this with his angels and saints in his glory singing his praise. How my heart longed for my husband and children to be with me in heaven one day! This vision consumed my heart and mind with both sweet sorrow and deep joy. As I stood with this grieving family around the body of their mother, who will someday stand resurrected at the heavenly throne, scales fell from my eyes. My obsession with my imperfections suddenly felt trivial. How could I worry about my weight on a scale in light of the *weight* of eternal glory? No longer did the voice of criticism and control speak from within. The lie was dispelled. Hope in our resurrection and the call to sainthood penetrated deeper than words could ever reach.

I wish I could tell you that I am always at total peace with my weight today. I confess I still desire to stand before a mirror and look at my body and find great joy and gratitude. Yet something *has* changed. Now, with deep conviction, I know that *I am lovely*. On good days, I proclaim that truth. On bad days, I struggle to enjoy a meal and silence the external voice that criticizes my imperfections. I have asked the Lord to take this last thorn from me. Perhaps that is exactly what he is doing as I conjure up the courage to share my struggle with other women. His power is being made perfect in my weakness. In the meantime, I stand in his truth. I declare that I do battle on the side of the Victor, and I claim that freedom in my life and for my lovely daughters. Most important, when I catch myself considering a new diet or wanting to lose a couple more pounds, I fall back on the truth that these things do not define me. What defines me is my Father's loving gaze and my Savior's merciful heart that claims me as his lovely, beloved daughter made for the weight of eternal glory.

## Take a Moment

1.  Pray with the following scripture from 2 Corinthians 12:8–10:

    > Three times I begged the Lord about this, that it might leave me, but he said to me, "My grace is sufficient for you, for power is made perfect in weakness." I will rather boast most gladly of my weaknesses, in order that the power of Christ may dwell with me. Therefore, I am content with weaknesses, insults, hardships, persecutions, and constraints, for the sake of Christ; for when I am weak, then I am strong.

    a. Read the scripture passage once and become familiar with the text.

    b. Slowly read the passage a second time.

    c. Very, very slowly read the passage a third time, paying attention to the words and phrases that rest in your heart. What is God speaking to you through this passage?

2. Can you relate to St. Paul in this passage, pleading with the Father to take away the thorn in his side? Are there any areas of habitual sin or affliction in your life that have caused you to lose hope? Or to doubt the Father's love?

3. How have you handled your own personal weakness? Do you believe that the Father can use *even our weakness* for his glory? Why or why not?

# Everything Is a Gift

## JUDY BAILEY

Alone, desperate, and cut off from God's love, in the darkest season of my life, I threw up an exasperated prayer into what felt like an abyss. Within weeks, the most unbelievable events transpired. This heart-wrenching plea for God to reveal himself to me brought me on a journey halfway around the world to a place I had never heard of. It was there that I began to learn the truth—that *I* am a beloved daughter.

I was brought up in a Protestant home, where both of my parents were active in our church. Desiring to grow deeper in my relationship with God, I allowed my tender heart to absorb every message preached from the pulpit. In early adolescence, I heard many fiery revival preachers who visited our community. Their hellfire-and-brimstone sermons shook me out of my innocent understanding of a *loving* and *compassionate* heavenly Father. Slowly, a different kind of God emerged in my heart and mind—a fearful God who was always watching and waiting for me to slip up and fall into sin so that he could send me to eternal damnation. This became the perfect setup for my crisis of faith later in life.

Fortunately, I had a loving and compassionate earthly father who sensed my struggles and doubts. Pulling me aside in those situations, he would share stories of his own early doubts, assuring me that God had always been there for him. My father was a genuine source of comfort to me. He showed me the true love of a father. Tragically and unexpectedly, he died a few weeks after my sixteenth birthday from a rare complication of an everyday virus.

Losing a father is always difficult, but at sixteen, I felt my world had been turned upside down. My father was the high school principal in our small community. He was highly respected. I was known as "Mr. Powell's daughter." After his death, I began to realize that I had lost more than just my father. In a real way, I had lost my identity in our community, school, and even in my own heart.

With the death of my father, I also watched fear overcome my mother. She had relied so heavily on him, and she had lost both her husband and—like me—her identity. As I witnessed her paralyzing fear and loneliness, I made a secret inner vow (see appendix I) that *I would never become that reliant on anyone, especially a man, in that way.*

Shortly after my father passed away, I set my sights on college and then a career in broadcast radio. Two years after graduation, I became a sales manager of a radio station. In another few years, I became the director of sales, and eventually the first female radio station market manager in our area. My goals were being realized one by one. I was independent, self-reliant, and successful. *I could take care of myself.*

Seven years into my career, I met Don. We dated six years before we married. Sadly, during our courtship my mother passed away. Her death left another deep hole in my heart. The months following her death, I experienced a profound sadness and loneliness for her. Yet there were times when I could feel her prayers and her presence, and a new stirring to allow God back into my life.

It was shortly after this that Don and I married. I was thirty-five, and he was forty-two years old. I was settled in my career, newly married, and ready for the natural next step—having a family. But a problem developed within *my* plan. During our first year of marriage, we conceived four times. Each time, I miscarried. I was heartbroken after the first loss, but I thought we would find the right doctor, the right procedure, the right solution, and we would be on our way to having the family we desired. I tried everything suggested, but after the fourth miscarriage, I was informed that while my body was able to conceive, it was unable to sustain life. Distraught by the news, I simply could not imagine a future without children.

With each pregnancy, I had prayed earnestly. I began to understand that the answer to my heart's desire was completely out of my control, dependent on someone or something other than me. The career that allowed me to feel in charge and self-reliant suddenly seemed empty and unimportant as I contemplated a future without children. *There was nothing I could do to change any of this.* Each prayer felt like it was hitting the ceiling. I heard nothing. I could not sense God's presence.

From the scary words planted in my heart at a tender age, it became easy for me to believe that an angry God, who had been watching my life of sin, had abandoned me in my time of desperate need. I began to wonder if any of what I had grown up believing was even true. These fears and questions sent a sick, cold chill through my heart, because I knew from those hellfire-and-brimstone sermons what would happen if I began to doubt the reality of Jesus as the Son of God.

After my fourth miscarriage and many weeks of excruciating inner turmoil, I concluded that there was no absolute way to know anything. I remember vividly the date when I was about to give up on God. It was April 17. I wrote in my journal, "God, if you want me, you are going to have to come down here and show me. Show me that you're real. Show me that you care. I'm struggling to hold on to my faith. I'm just not sure anymore." This desperate prayer was a pivotal turning point in my life. From the moment I wrote that prayer in my journal, the doors of heaven opened to my cries, and God's grace began to move.

Within a few short weeks, Terri, a coworker, returned from Medjugorje, a place in former Yugoslavia where six children received daily apparitions of the Blessed Mother. In my Protestant world, I had no knowledge or understanding of apparitions, so on her first day back, I asked Terri if she had enjoyed her "vacation." With tears in her eyes, she suggested that I visit her home after work, so that she could share some of the things she had experienced. I quickly invited her into my office, where she began to speak.

*Amazing* does not even begin to describe the miraculous stories Terri relayed to me. At one point, she told me of how the Blessed Mother had appeared to her and two companions one evening outside St. James Church in Medjugorje. The Blessed Mother spoke gently to each of them and thanked them for coming. She then spoke directly to Terri, presenting her with a special mission. She communicated to Terri that she knew seven people who were searching for her Son and asked her to invite them to Medjugorje during a specific week in August. Then Terri became very quiet and began to cry. Looking at me intently, she said, "Judy, she gave me your name." My heart was pierced. I immediately recalled my prayer. In an instant my heart knew what I longed to know. Heaven was real, God was real, and the mother of Jesus was calling me to come "taste and see that the LORD is good" (Ps 34:9).

Four months later, my husband and I were on a plane to Medjugorje with Terri and a group of fifteen others. While I was there, so many knots were undone in my heart. I began to see the unraveling of these knots one by one just as in the beautiful image of Mary, Undoer of Knots (see appendix II).

During our trip, my husband had a series of life-changing visions. The first was an image of my mother sitting at the feet of Mary with her arms around the Blessed Mother's waist. My mother turned her gaze gently toward my husband, and with a knowing look she smiled. When he shared this vision with me, it gave me great comfort. I had deep regrets that I had not been by my mother's side when she died. By the time I arrived at the hospital, she was in a coma. We made the decision to take her off life support once her brain activity stopped. It was one of the most difficult decisions I have ever made, and I chose not to stay in the room. After years of carrying this intense regret and guilt, I was finally set free by Don's vision.

Later, my husband received another incredible vision, in which Jesus untangled some deeply rooted lies within his heart. Jesus also gave Don several messages for those in our group, and he was told that we would each receive a gift. Some would receive their gift while in Medjugorje, and others once they returned home. Before we left Medjugorje, Don disclosed to Terri that my gift would be a *son*. Within two weeks of returning home, I found out I was pregnant. The following April, I gave birth to a healthy baby boy!

It had taken me many years to acknowledge and unpack all of the knots that were undone by Our Blessed Mother in Medjugorje. A beautiful thread of motherly love was woven throughout the fabric of this profound experience. Jesus' mother wanted me to know her Son *as he truly was*—kind, compassionate, and someone who was not angry but knew every sorrow and pain I had carried from losing my dad, my mother, and all my babies. While he knew my sins, God wasn't waiting to punish me. No, he wanted to show me his compassion. My husband's vision of my mother smiling at him with her arms around Mary removed the guilt and shame I had been bound with for years. And when Mary called me to Medjugorje *by name*, she opened the door for me to understand that my true identity was found in being a beloved daughter of my Father in heaven. Through the struggles of miscarriage and then the gift of my son, the knot of self-sufficiency unraveled as I learned that everything—*everything*—is a gift of God's grace and I can do *nothing* without him.

# *Take a Moment*

1. Pray with the following scripture from Psalm 34:5–9:

> I sought the LORD, and he answered me,
> delivered me from all my fears.
> Look to him and be radiant,
> and your faces may not blush for shame.
> This poor one cried out, and the LORD heard,
> and from all his distress he saved him.
> The angel of the LORD encamps
> around those who fear him, and he saves them.
> Taste and see that the LORD is good;
> blessed is the stalwart one who takes refuge in him.

   a. Read the scripture passage once and become familiar with the text.

   b. Slowly read the passage a second time.

   c. Very, very slowly read the passage a third time, paying attention to the words and phrases that rest in your heart. What is the Holy Spirit speaking to you through this passage?

2. What stirs in your heart when you think of God as your compassionate Father who knows your needs and comes to rescue you when you cry out to him?

3. Are there areas in your life where you need rescuing? If so, what prevents you from crying out to your heavenly Father for help?

# Inner Healing Prayer

## DAUGHTER IDENTITY

## BOB SCHUCHTS

As you engage in this meditative and contemplative prayer experience, allow the Holy Spirit to lead you. Pause after each step to record your experiences in a journal.

Meditation "is a prayerful quest engaging thought, imagination, emotion, and desire. Its goal is to make our own in faith the subject considered, by confronting it with the reality of our own life" (*CCC* 2723). Contemplative prayer is an experience of being led by the Holy Spirit into the mysteries of Christ's life (*CCC* 2715). As we grow in union with him, and with the Holy Family, he redeems and restores every aspect of our lives and identity (see *CCC* 518–520).

1.  Ask the Holy Spirit to show you the specific and general ways you were loved and blessed as a daughter by your mother and father, your grandparents, aunts and uncles, and any other parental figures in your life. Record these reflections in your

journal and write a prayer of thanksgiving for these gifts of love and blessing.

2.  Ask the Holy Spirit to reveal how and when you were wounded in your identity as daughter, in any of those relationships. Where was love missing? Let yourself experience what it was like for you to be a daughter in your family.

3.  Ask the Holy Spirit to reveal to you the knots that have kept your heart bound as a daughter. What are the deeply rooted lies underlying these knots? Write them in your journal.

4.  Contemplate being a daughter of Mary and Joseph (in union with Jesus). Receive their blessing, affirming, nurturing, teaching, and modeling love for you. Let it unfold. In your imagination, watch how they relate to you and listen to what they speak to you. See how they love each other, and receive the overflow of that love. Write in your prayer journal what you saw, thought, felt, and desired.

5.  Ask the Holy Spirit to reveal to you the truth about your identity as a beloved daughter in any areas where the lies took root in your heart. Record these truths in your journal.

6.  Close with a prayer to the Father, thanking him for blessing your identity as his beloved daughter.

# PART II

## *Sister*

### BOB SCHUCHTS

Whether or not you have siblings, you *are* a sister. You became a sister when you entered this world. We all share a common humanity and have the same Creator. Apart from siblings, you may have cousins or friends who were like brothers and sisters. In addition, Jesus is your brother (see Heb 2:11; Rom 8:16–17) and Mary is your sister. You are also a sister within the whole communion of saints and with every living person.

By God's design, brothers and sisters are meant to share life together, basking in the love of their parents and respecting and celebrating each other's uniqueness. Siblings teach us how to share, compete, support, and cooperate. They are often our playmates and confidants. When loved well by siblings, sisters feel safe and develop a sense of belonging and trust. They learn to serve and confide in each other. In what ways did you receive these gifts of sisterhood as God intended? In what ways was your identity as sister confounded by wounds and lies?

In this part, Danielle, Colleen, and Carolyn share their personal reflections on what it is like being a sister. As you read their stories, I encourage you to think about your own experience of

being a sister. At the end of this part, you will have an opportunity
to bring to prayer all you have experienced as a sister—as a way of
receiving a deeper blessing and healing in your authentic identity
as a beloved sister.

# Warrior Sisterhood

## DANIELLE CHODOROWSKI

I was born into a sisterhood. I am one of three daughters to my mom, who is also one of three girls, whose mother, my grandma, is one of two girls. Female genetics were a powerhouse in my family. Growing up, we were affirmed, empowered, and encouraged to be phenomenal women. These sentiments promoted independence, comparison, and competition, yet deep within me I desired camaraderie, confidence, and a sense of belonging. In grade school I longed for close friends to talk with, play with, and share life with, including choreographing dance routines in my living room to the latest pop music hit. In junior high, I remember being quite awkward with my frizzy hair, braces, tortoiseshell glasses, and untrendy clothes. I begged my mom to buy me a pair of white Keds and contact lenses so I would fit in, but to no avail. Instead, I received heart-wrenching ridicule from other girls and was the subject of mean notes passed in class and gossip on the playground. I even recall one girl slapping me across the face just to look cool in front of her friends.

Immense damage was done to my fragile heart during these years, especially as I watched the friends I did have stand by and say nothing in the face of these taunts. I believed the lies born of these traumatic experiences, which were reinforced again and again. *I am alone. I cannot trust others. I am unseen and unneeded.* By God's grace, these painful experiences didn't bury me in a deep depression or hopelessness. Nevertheless, the core group of friends I journeyed with through the teen years never really knew my carefully guarded heart. I am not sure even I knew my own heart.

As I prepared to leave for college, the Lord began calling my name. This encounter gradually transformed my heart. An image that has stuck with me for many years is that of an old, dried-up stone well. At the bottom of the well lies a thick layer of dead leaves, moss, sludge, and decay. As water slowly fills the well again, the layers on the bottom rise to the surface. The layers of decay have to be removed and cleared in order to get to the fresh, life-giving water.

Before I knew Christ, my heart was much like that empty well. My brokenness, sin, and wounds from the sins of others formed a thick layer over my heart. Gently, the Holy Spirit poured new life into me, and I experienced the tremendous love and mercy of the Lord. It was truly transformational. I began to see myself in his eyes. The light of Christ gradually penetrated those deep places of brokenness and pain in my heart. As the light shone brighter, the Lord brought many tender hidden wounds and sins to the surface for him to heal. Layer by layer, he called me closer to his heart. He patiently waited for me to be ready and willing to say yes to this healing too.

My relationship with Christ blossomed and grew in the midst of a community of friends who were also on the journey to know and love the Lord and the Church. We became disciples, running the race together. The foundation of these friendships was Christ. He brought us together and knit a strong bond. Through this particular experience, the Lord began to address the lies I had believed from a young age and gave me a safe space to trust and be vulnerable with these friends.

As the years passed, I became very close to one friend in particular. She and I shared life's joys, sufferings, and struggles. We visited each other, did ministry work together, celebrated each other's victories, marriages, and children, and grieved each other's sorrows. Unexpectedly, she cut off all communication. Phone calls went unanswered. Emails bounced back. Complete silence. It felt like the unexpected death of a dear friend.

Seizing this opportunity, the enemy of my heart whispered the old familiar words: *Get over it, you were a fool to trust her. You are not needed. You are too much. You are all alone.* Brick by brick, the wall of protection rose around my heart. Life moved on. My heart continued to bear the burden of self-reliance and loneliness.

Less than a year after this break with my close friend, my husband, Dave, and I relocated from the Ohio Valley to Florida. As we settled our family in a new town and community, I kept busy homeschooling our four young children. I was happy to be at home and not have to engage and build community. I was convinced that at the age of thirty-six, it was impossible to build solid friendships. I assumed that all women my age already had their established group of friends and that, again, I was not needed or wanted. To my surprise, an acquaintance graciously welcomed our family to the area. She would call and check in on us, encouraged us to get involved with the local Catholic homeschool group and co-op, and invited our brood over to watch football with her family. It was exciting, but honestly, I was skeptical, convinced it was pity or just a fleeting gesture. All the while, my heart ached with loneliness and fear.

One day during my prayer time, my heart was repeatedly drawn to Isaiah 43. It stood out as a declaration proclaimed to the deep recesses of my heart. First, God reminded me that I am his—his beloved, his creation, and precious in his sight. Then he spoke the resounding truth that I am not alone, in any circumstance I may face.

> Do not fear, for I have redeemed you;
>> I have called you by name: you are mine.
> When you pass through waters, I will be with you;
>> through rivers, you shall not be swept away.

> When you walk through fire, you shall not be burned,
>     nor will flames consume you.

The Lord had my attention! The Holy Spirit moved deep within, speaking words of love that I longed to hear. He declared that I was precious, honored, loved, and safe.

> Because you are precious in my eyes
>     and honored, and I love you,
> I give people in return for you
>     and nations in exchange for your life.
> Fear not, for I am with you

Emboldened by his mighty Word, he proclaimed his power and majesty. All things are possible for him, the Lord!

> I am the LORD, your Holy One,
>     the creator of Israel, your King.
> Thus says the LORD,
>     who makes a way in the sea,
>     a path in the mighty waters.

And then he spoke prophetically to my heart. He was about to do something new and make a way where there was none before. "Pay attention and be watchful!"

> Remember not the events of the past,
>     the things of long ago consider not;
> See, I am doing something new!
>     Now it springs forth, do you not perceive it?
> In the wilderness I make a way,
>     in the wasteland, rivers.
>     (Is 43:1–2, 4–5, 15–16, 18–19)

I still get chills reading this beautiful passage. With these words, the mortar in between the bricks in my wall of protection turned to dust. The bricks, however, stood. It was up to me to walk into a place of freedom. It was up to me to take a step toward trust and vulnerability. Not surprisingly, within a few days, the Lord gave me such an opportunity.

The same acquaintance asked me to join her and another friend to pray for some specific intentions and healing. From the moment we joined in prayer, I felt a deep, abiding peace and joy. God's presence was tangible as he worked a mighty healing in this beautiful woman before us. In that sacred space there was a light and freedom that ignited something within me that had been hidden for so long. As we walked to our cars, I quietly asked for prayers specifically for my loneliness and ability to connect with Dave. They immediately stopped walking, took my hands, and prayed with me on the sidewalk. As they prayed, the wall of self-protection crumbled. I was overwhelmed by an all-encompassing peace.

This moment of prayer led not only to true friendships of sisterhood but also to the gift of our fifth child. The fear of trusting others had seeped from friendships to my marriage. As times of stress entered our family life, the greater the divide became. The impact of this breakthrough prayer and acceptance of the truth of Christ was transformational. With Christ as my protection, I felt safe to be who he created me to be. With great joy I can say that the friendships that followed are some of the most beautiful fruits of our time in that community.

Since that time of prayer, my heart has changed. A deep bond of friendship formed among the three of us, along with two other amazing women. We have promised to journey together as sisters in Christ. These are my warrior sisters. Like the men who carried their paralyzed friend to Jesus to be healed (Lk 5:18), we are committed to championing one another through every season of life. We have walked through sickness, death, infertility, unexpected pregnancy, miscarriage, adoptions, and all the joys and victories of life. There is a sincere celebration of how the Lord is working in each of us. The love and witness of these women testify to me of the goodness of God. They speak truth and call out beauty and goodness. The fruit of this type of sisterhood is changing the world moment to moment.

## Take a Moment

1.  Pray with the following scripture from Isaiah 43:1–2:

    > Do not fear, for I have redeemed you;
    >     I have called you by name: you are mine.
    > When you pass through waters, I will be with you;
    >     through rivers, you shall not be swept away.
    > When you walk through fire, you shall not be burned,
    >     nor will flames consume you.

    a.  Read the scripture passage once and become familiar with the text.
    b.  Slowly read the passage a second time.
    c.  Very, very slowly read the passage a third time, paying attention to the words and phrases that rest in your heart. What is God speaking to you through this passage?
2.  As you reflect on this scripture, think of Jesus as your brother, who is walking with you through all the events of your life. Do you believe that he knows you by name and that he is with you when you pass through troubled waters?
3.  What deeply rooted lies about you as a sister make this hard to believe?

# My True Blues

## COLLEEN NIXON

Many assume that children in big families are close and spend all their time with their "built-in best friends." This wasn't the case in my family. I was born fourth in a family of five children. I have two older brothers, an older sister, and a younger sister. While we were blessed with wonderfully loving parents, who established a safe place for us to foster our dreams, we rarely spent any time together. As a child, I believed my brothers and sisters did not like me.

Looking back, I see now that the divide between us began after my oldest brother was diagnosed with cancer. I had just finished kindergarten when my parents very calmly sat my brother, sister, and me down to let us know that our oldest brother was sick. I was too young to understand what they were communicating. I only remember feeling excited to be shipped off to my favorite cousins in south Florida while my parents took my big brother across the country to visit numerous pediatric cancer specialists. When we all arrived back home, I quickly learned this sickness was something that wasn't going away.

Along with the obvious physical changes of hair loss and the ghostly pale face, there was a significant interior change in him that my feminine heart felt very deeply, even at my young age. His anger toward the disease that threatened to take his life spilled over into all of our lives and greatly affected our relationships with him and one another. As this young teenage boy experienced the onset of pubescent hormones and a loss of control, he also battled cancer. Each round of chemotherapy required drug after drug to be pumped into his body. The wretched side effect was hours of vomiting in the bathroom right across the hall from my bedroom. He was in a constant state of pain and physical exhaustion, which forced him into an understandable place of immense impatience. He became stone cold and distant. I quickly learned that if I didn't honor the distance, the blowup was as lethal as a grenade. The cancer in his body was becoming a cancer in our home.

One particular incident has replayed in my head hundreds of times. My mom had asked me to take my brother some soup and crackers on a tray. I was delighted to serve and help my "sick" brother in this way. I quickly put on an apron, picked up the tray, and sang all the way down the long hall in our ranch-style home, pretending I was Cinderella. By the time I reached my brother's doorway, his blood was boiling. I was immediately scolded and silenced by his rage. It was in this moment that I recall the knot of rejection tangle my heart and make its way into our relationship. To my five-year-old self, this moment communicated a lie from the evil one that *I was an unlovable annoyance.* I believed that I was stupid for thinking that I could help him feel better. What is more, my voice (my passion) needed to be silenced in his presence.

Believing this lie made me afraid to be myself around him. This fear eventually seeped into my relationship with my other siblings. I made an inner vow (see appendix I) from a place of self-protection that *I would not be vulnerable or show my real self.* From this place of rejection, a *fear* of rejection was born, as was another inner vow. I vowed *never to let anyone feel disregarded or rejected by me.* I made it my personal quest to be kind and loving to each person I met. This vow, as well intended as it seemed, wasn't made in freedom. Ultimately it stunted me from facing the real pain in my heart. Instead, I faced outward, seeking to maintain as many friends as possible. I started to look at friendships as opportunities to show myself (and my siblings) that I was not annoying. People actually *wanted* to be around me.

I attended a small Catholic grade school. The atmosphere fostered a natural feeling of family among my peers. While there were many cliques in my grade, I was welcomed into each group, and I became skilled at diffusing any drama and figuring out everyone's interests. I took mental notes on each person's likes and dislikes as a way of being in control. I would allow myself to feel close and be trusted, but I avoided conflict. I wouldn't share parts of me that could possibly offend another's point of view or make them upset with me.

As I approached my teenage years, I managed to make a couple of real friends who knew every part of me. I secretly held those friends above all the rest in my heart and called them my *true blues*. Out of love for me, they tried to be like siblings to me. Yet at the end of the day, my ache for the attention of my brothers and sisters was still there. This reality was heightened by the fact that all my true blues were close with their siblings. They didn't need me in the way that I needed them. They shared a deeper connection with their siblings than they did with me. I wasn't the first person they went to to share the exciting news that they had landed a part in the big play or that the guy they liked had a crush on them. My knot of rejection pulled tighter as I knew deep down that my true blues would never care for me as much as I cared for them.

By the time I reached my senior year of high school, my older siblings had all left home. Just my youngest sister and I remained. We were not close. The rejection I experienced from my older sister was thrown at my younger sister.

Unlike my grade-school class, my high-school class numbered close to four hundred kids. It was almost impossible to know everyone. However, I became involved in so many different clubs and organizations that over the course of four years I made many long-term connections with my classmates. On Senior Award Night, when my name was called for the honor of "Best Personality," I was shocked. *Me?* While I relished the fact that I had avoided rejection and adapted parts of myself to make others feel comfortable, I couldn't help but wonder if this label was true. After all, my own siblings did not see this side of me.

When I entered college, I found myself back at square one. I pursued friendships with people of every background and watched as they fell in love with whatever part of me they hoped to see. Yet deep down, I was looking for a deeper connection. At the same time, my older sister, who was a senior in college and lived across the country, started to pursue *me,* her *sister,* as a *friend.* I was completely surprised by her interest in me at first, and I didn't know how to respond. I thought it was weird that she was being nice to me. I learned later that she had started her own healing journey, untying the knots that tangled her own heart. By her simple example of openness and vulnerability, she invited me into a deeper relationship and deeper freedom. With each phone call, email, care package, CD, or sweet note in my mailbox, the knots started to unravel. The lies stopped strangling my heart. Through her *friendship* I experienced her love of me as a *sister.* It was such a gift to finally share a desire for real relationship with each other. Because of my older sister's loving example, I began seeking out relationship with my younger sister. The blessing of invitation and receptivity snowballed through our entire family, including all my sibling relationships. I found that the more vulnerable I was, the more freedom and happiness I had in their presence. They needed the *real* me—every shade of me. With joy, they welcomed it. The lie that I was annoying and stupid was a place of darkness finally illuminated by a new and deep truth. My brothers and sisters love me for *who I am.*

I can see now that the rejection I felt from my siblings as a child stemmed from the chaotic dynamic and pain of my brother's illness. We weren't intentionally rejecting one another; we were just coping. Glory be to God; the oncology world deemed my brother cured five years after the initial diagnosis. While it took us siblings a bit longer to recover, I can say with confidence that we too have healed.

I once heard my mom say she raised five incredibly independent children who weren't particularly cohesive. I agreed with her then, but I don't have to anymore. Today my siblings are the friends I always longed for . . . my real *true blues.*

## Take a Moment

1.  Pray with the following scripture from Sirach 6:14–17:

    > Faithful friends are a sturdy shelter;
    >> whoever finds one finds a treasure.
    >
    > Faithful friends are beyond price,
    >> no amount can balance their worth.
    >
    > Faithful friends are life-saving medicine;
    >> those who fear God will find them.
    >
    > Those who fear the Lord enjoy stable friendship,
    >> for as they are, so will their neighbors be.

    a.  Read the scripture passage once and become familiar with the text.

    b.  Slowly read the passage a second time.

    c.  Very, very slowly read the passage a third time, paying attention to the words and phrases that rest in your heart. What is God speaking to you through this passage?

2.  Do you have friends or siblings with whom you can truly be yourself? Explain.

3.  Have you experienced rejection in friendship that prevents you from being vulnerable with others? Explain.

# Discord to Harmony

## CAROLYN PIERCE BROWN

"Absolutely ethereal beauty . . . stunning! But . . . whatever happened to these lovely singers? . . . It would be wonderful to hear more."[1]

My heart aches when I read the rave review on Amazon for an album my sisters and I recorded together called *Songs for Life*. It makes me want to cyberstalk the reviewer and say, "Hello, thank you for the incredible compliment, but do you really want to know what has happened to us after our success? Life happened! We have tried so many times to record our blend of harmonies again, but it just never came together."

The simple act of singing with my sisters required a wholeness and harmony that for many years did not exist between us. While we grew up in a Catholic home with parents who love Jesus, we were a fantastic blend of incredible love and dysfunctional complexity.

Growing up, I often resorted to emotional withdrawal. Conflict typically played out in my head long after the argument ended. Most of my family seemed to handle conflict through angry, explosive words. I preferred to harbor my negative emotions deep within. Perhaps the words of Elsa from *Frozen* summarized my approach to relationship best: *conceal, don't feel.*[2]

45

Given my melancholic tendencies, music was a gift of relief as it transcended the words I struggled to speak. Beethoven reflected, "Don't only practice your art, but force your way into its secrets."[3] After *Songs for Life,* I delved into a master's in music program, figuring it would offer greater tools to unlock the secrets of my art.

Life started to unravel during my final year in graduate school. I faced a series of traumatic events far beyond the early conflicts at home. Newly married and expecting, I lost our first baby through miscarriage. While blessed to conceive again, I delivered my son only a month before my graduation. The delivery was a natural birth that resulted in painful physical trauma that took weeks to heal. As my body was healing, I feebly stood in the back of the room at my graduation ceremony, cradling my newborn. We were so financially strapped that the thought of spending money for a cap and gown had sidelined me at my own graduation.

Within two weeks of that event, we found ourselves preparing for a move for a new job. On moving day, my husband discovered eighteen frantic messages on our answering machine. My father had been injured in a horrible accident, was subsequently flown to a trauma unit, and was now lying in a coma. His life was hanging in the balance.

I recall standing in the middle of our new place surrounded by boxes as the news sank in. With my newborn in my arms, I was almost too tired to stand. An ocean of tears swelled furiously inside of me. I remember feeling emotionally disabled, unable to let the tears fall. They resolutely lodged just under the surface. My overwhelming grief sank into a deeper and darker space. Instead of crying, I ran to the bathroom and threw up.

While our family attempted to make sense of the accident, we continued to receive a steady stream of feedback that *Songs for Life* was helping critically ill patients around the country recover. Several times over the months and years, we heard that women were using it as their soundtrack while giving birth. The life-and-death significance of our music was not lost on us. We, too, played the CD for my father while he lay unconscious in his hospital bed. Miraculously, he emerged from his coma. Still, we knew he had a long and uncertain recovery ahead.

Traveling miles with babies in tow, my sisters and I made a few dogged attempts to record our harmonies again in honor of our father. No matter how hard we tried, it just never came together.

I continued to sing regularly for work. I mostly sang in very formal liturgical settings, where the strength of my emotions transferred comfortably into musical perfectionism. I was also serious about my spiritual life, regularly going to Mass, Confession, and adoration and attending retreats. I read scripture and sought the best spiritual direction I could find. Over the years, these resources were a lifeline, allowing me the space to touch Jesus. Yet, buried beneath the surface, my heart had knotted cords of indescribable hopelessness, powerlessness, and pain.

During these long years after my father's accident, my sisters and I experienced other significant hardships. When we mixed our collective pain, the relationships sometimes became a recipe for disaster. We all tasted the dysfunction over Christmas five years ago. One of my sisters had endured multiple late-term miscarriages. The new and exhausting adoption process she had begun stretched her emotions thin. My other sister endured several episodes of depression. Newly postpartum with my fifth child, I operated in an overwhelmed state and coped by taking on too many responsibilities in an effort to control the powerlessness I felt. The relational dynamics that holiday were damaging. Rather than becoming a bridge through shared experience, our sufferings caused discord. In retrospect, I can see that we each had a reasonable desire to be understood and supported by one another. What happened instead was a triangle of pain projection. As conversations became heated, I gave in to the familiar despair I had embraced as a child: *conceal, don't feel.*

A few days after, we found ourselves singing together for a family wedding that we had committed to months before. While I was skilled in performing over my internal pain, the heaviness of it all felt suffocating. I doubted if I would ever desire to sing with them again.

That January, for my birthday, I asked my sisters for the gift of three months of space and silence. Emotionally depleted and drained from having a baby, I thought this would be a way to regain a sense of safety and strength to cope with life. My sisters were understandably hurt by my request. Of course, the time apart did not help me feel any less overwhelmed.

When we did come together again, our gatherings were less dramatic than that one devastating Christmas visit. This was in part because we had kids to care for, wine to drink, and distractions to keep the deeper hurts at bay. Plus, we had also all experienced some relief from the hardships that had previously felt so acute. Adoption brought healing and hope to one sister. The other had received some new freedom from clinical depression. I was slowly maturing in learning not to take responsibility for situations that weren't mine to fix. While our father's brain injury remained a harsh reality, our mother's heroic witness of care and fidelity was healing for all of us.

While my healing journey has been very gradual and gentle, I did experience a definitive moment of truth. It occurred during a personal encounter with God through scripture. I was on retreat with a handful of other women when my fragile heart somehow felt safe enough to receive light in some dark places. I was invited to spend a morning praying through the story of the hemorrhaging woman in the Gospel of Mark (5:25–34).

My heart started to pound as the sacred words jumped off the page and into my own living reality. Like the hemorrhaging woman, I was desperate for a solution to my suffering. After exhausting every option, the woman must have had some serious pent-up frustration. I imagined her feeling powerless in her pain and withdrawing to her inner cell. I wondered what lies she believed about herself after enduring years of pain and isolation. In her pain, she reached out to Jesus.

I had read this scripture many times over the years, but this time I heard something more. When Jesus asked, "Who has touched my clothes?" it occurred to me that I had run away after touching Jesus, like the woman in the story. I wanted healing but preferred not to be known. Yet Jesus had been relentlessly pursuing me for an intimate connection. Then it hit me: simply touching Jesus was not the end of the woman's story. It was not the end of mine. How could I still be emotionally hemorrhaging after touching him so many times? I realized that Jesus desired more than a miraculous healing. He wants us to feel *pursued*. So I asked myself, *Can I allow Jesus to pursue me? What would it feel like to be* found *by him?* This thought gripped me. After all, it is only after Jesus' pursuit that the woman becomes undone. The moment he finds her, she no longer has to conceal her pent-up feelings. *I no longer have to hide my pent-up feelings.* All those years of suffering in silence had left me bleeding internally. In choosing not to acknowledge my pain (even to myself), I remained bound by it. Holding my pain in had negatively affected my relationship with God and all those I loved. It had caused a wedge in my closest relationships.

I suddenly understood that letting myself become undone in Jesus' presence means lifting the veil on my grief and my other knotted-up emotions, even if it all looks and feels like a bloody mess. Jesus can handle my mess.

I've revisited these insights over and over again, becoming mindful of the places I am hemorrhaging and intentionally allowing the pain to rise to the surface so I can effectively grieve life's hurts and heartaches. This past year, when my maternal grandmother passed away and I stood with my heart laid bare next to my sisters, singing for her funeral, I allowed the pain to rise to the surface. Deep stirrings of regret and longing swelled up in me. I clearly saw the layers of discord and unforgiveness between us. I desired a restored connection.

In light of this revelation, I asked my sisters to fly to Florida to celebrate my birthday with a weekend retreat and one day in a recording studio. This was our chance to be together and record again. As I prepared for the weekend, I allowed myself to pore over music we had once loved to sing together. Initially I was nervous, afraid that painful emotions would drown the potential for harmony, both relationally and musically. One talk on the retreat, however, highlighted the strong, healthy relationship between Mary and Elizabeth. The speaker shared about the significance of women showing up for one another. It was a powerful theme.

In past visits, my sisters and I have wallowed in memories of agonizing resentment for not supporting one another in times of need. This time, we relaxed and sipped wine together, remembering moments when we had shown up for one another, like Mary for Elizabeth. We dubbed these "Visitation Moments." We recalled enormous financial gifts in difficult times. We remembered food and love delivered during hardships. We recognized all the care we offered one another through the trials of miscarriages and still-births. We intentionally focused on memories of strong connection and devoted support. It was incredibly healing. The perfect end to the weekend came after Communion the following day, when we were asked to sing in harmony together in front of the entire group of captivated women.

Early the next day, the three of us headed to the recording studio. Beloved music and arrangements we had held in our hearts for almost twenty years finally fell into place. Like our first recording, I know our music will reach all those it is intended to touch. We are calling it *Songs for Life: Restoration*. Discord will not have the final word. My sisters and I are harmonizing again.

# Take a Moment

1.  Pray with the following scripture from Mark 5:25–34:

    There was a woman afflicted with hemorrhages for
    twelve years. She had suffered greatly at the hands of
    many doctors and had spent all that she had. Yet she
    was not helped but only grew worse. She had heard
    about Jesus and came up behind him in the crowd and
    touched his cloak. She said, "If I but touch his clothes,
    I shall be cured." Immediately her flow of blood dried
    up. She felt in her body that she was healed of her afflic-
    tion. Jesus, aware at once that power had gone out from
    him, turned around in the crowd and asked, "Who has
    touched my clothes?" But his disciples said to him, "You
    see how the crowd is pressing upon you, and yet you
    ask, 'Who touched me?'" And he looked around to see
    who had done it. The woman, realizing what had hap-
    pened to her, approached in fear and trembling. She fell
    down before Jesus and told him the whole truth. He said
    to her, "Daughter, your faith has saved you. Go in peace
    and be cured of your affliction."

    a.  Read the scripture passage once and become familiar with
        the text.
    b.  Slowly read the passage a second time.
    c.  Very, very slowly read the passage a third time, paying
        attention to the words and phrases that rest in your heart.
        What is God speaking to you through this passage?

2.  Have you ever had an experience with your siblings or friends
    in which you felt as though you exhausted every effort and were
    getting nowhere? If so, explain.

3.  Are there any areas in your identity as sister where Jesus may
    be pursuing you but your back is turned away? What might it
    feel like to turn toward him?

# Inner Healing Prayer

## SISTER IDENTITY

## BOB SCHUCHTS

As you engage in this meditative and contemplative prayer experience, allow the Holy Spirit to lead you. Pause after each step to record your experiences in a journal.

1. Ask the Holy Spirit to show you the specific and general ways you were loved and affirmed as a sister by your siblings, cousins, friends, and peers. Record these reflections in your journal and write a prayer of thanksgiving for these gifts of love and affirmation.
2. Ask the Holy Spirit to reveal to you how and when you were wounded in your identity as a sister. You may have memories, feelings, or thoughts. Let yourself experience what it was like for you to be a sister in your family and peer group. Record what you experience in your journal.
3. Ask the Holy Spirit to reveal to you the knots that have kept your heart from living freely in your identity as a sister. What

are the lies underlying these knots? Write down the knots and
the lies in your journal.

4.  Ask the Holy Spirit to allow you to experience life with Jesus in
    the Holy Family. By Baptism you are united with Jesus. Con-
    template having Jesus as your brother and Mary as your sister.
    Receive their love and affirmation as a healing of your wounds.
    In your sanctified imagination, watch how they relate to each
    other and to you. Listen to what they speak to you. See how
    they love each other and invite you into that circle of love and
    belonging. Write in your prayer journal what you saw, thought,
    felt, and desired.

5.  Ask the Holy Spirit to reveal to you the truth about your identi-
    ty as a sister in any areas where the lies took root in your heart.
    Record these truths in your journal.

6.  Finally, ask Jesus and Mary to untie the knots that were formed
    in your relationships with siblings, other relatives, and friends.
    Come back in a few weeks and record how things have changed
    regarding these knots.

7.  Close with a prayer of thanksgiving to Jesus for treating you
    well as his sister.

# PART III

## *Bride*

### BOB SCHUCHTS

Whether or not you are married, you are a bride. Christ is your eternal Bridegroom. He delights in you. He nourishes and cherishes you, beyond the capacity of any boyfriend or husband. However, you may have had experiences with men that have left you feeling alone and less than desirable. You may not have been chosen (yet) for marriage. You may have been rejected or cheated on in dating or marriage. Or perhaps you have a good marriage but still desire more. Any of these experiences may have tarnished your identity as bride.

Whether in dating, courtship, or marriage, or perhaps as a consecrated woman, you have the desire to be loved fully, freely, faithfully, and fruitfully. In God's design, brides are meant to be cherished, nourished, and intimately loved. Have you received these gifts as God intended?

In this part, Kristen, Lisa, Jen, and Jeannie share their personal reflections on what it was like living into their identity as bride. As you read their stories, I encourage you to think about your own experience of being a bride. At the end of this part, you will have an opportunity to bring to prayer all you have experienced as a bride—as a way of receiving a deeper blessing and healing in your authentic identity as a beloved bride.

# Ravish My Heart

## KRISTEN BLAKE

"You have ravished my heart, my sister, my bride, you have ravished my heart with a glance of your eyes" (Sg 4:9 RSV). From the time I was old enough to understand desire, I had an ache to know this kind of love. In reality, I felt anything but beautiful and lovable. By the time I was twelve, the many arrows that pierced my fragile heart had convinced me that I was not desirable or worth pursuing. Under the spell of this lie, I began to grasp at even the smallest hint of love's fulfillment.

In high school, this took the form of "hooking up" (making out) with boys I liked. Left with a broken heart, I realized that my beauty did not ravish them. I wasn't worth fighting for.

About two weeks before high school graduation, I started talking to this one particular boy. While neither of us expected it to go further than just another hookup, we ended up dating all summer. As the new school year approached, I feared he would find a better beauty away at college, so I slept with him in order to keep him. Holding on tight, I refused to let go.

After six years and *many* issues, we were still together and utterly miserable. We suffered from a lack of communication, a lack of respect, and a lack of trust. We lived out our relationship in lust, fear, deceit, shame, and anxiety. I began to wonder if there was more to love than this.

With this thought, I felt new conviction to stop having sex with him. You can only imagine the strain that put on our already unstable relationship. It became the topic of our arguments. He would say, "We love each other, and we should have sex to express that love." I would say, "If you really loved me, you could show me in other ways." I wanted him to love all of me, but I felt like he was saying, *I don't want to love your mind, or your heart, or your soul, just your body.*

Removing sex from our relationship allowed me to see things more clearly. All of our problems rose to the surface. That is when God knocked the wind out of me. I was given a book on the theology of the body titled *Good News about Sex and Marriage*, by Christopher West.[1] Every lie I had come to believe about love was exposed through this book. The truth was transforming. After six years of living in denial, I was finally honest with myself. I was not fulfilled. I was being used. I was using him. We were settling for less than what we were created for.

For the first time, I asked God for direction in my relationship. I begged him to show me a clear sign of what to do. To my amazement, he did. He immediately spoke to me via another person and made his answer crystal clear. I was to end the relationship.

This was by far the most agonizing decision I have ever made. Time and sexual intimacy had forged a strong attachment, and parting ways was excruciating. One of the hardest parts was facing the possibility of being alone. I feared I might be alone for the rest of my life. I also feared that I would never find someone who would love all of me.

Mixed with the pain, however, was a sense of relief. I did not have to live in the turmoil of an unhealthy relationship any longer. I knew God had taken me out of it for a reason, although I wasn't quite sure where I would go from there. At the age of twenty-four, I was out of college and in a workplace with only women. I had no easy way to meet and get to know men. I sought this interaction in the bar scene, but that quickly left me feeling empty and unfulfilled. Instead, I began to dive deeper into St. John Paul II's theology of the body.[2] The more I read, the more I realized the truth. This teaching spoke deeply to my heart.

I was compelled to go to Confession for the first time in fifteen years. To say it was a weight off my shoulders is a gross understatement. I also spoke to my parents about all that I had kept hidden for the six long years my boyfriend and I were together. I felt so free! The shame that had kept me bound for so long was gone. I was new.

One book I read spoke about the gift of single life. The author unpacked this verse from Corinthians: "An unmarried woman or a virgin is anxious about the things of the Lord, so that she may be holy in both body and spirit" (1 Cor 7:34). It was a great insight for me to realize that my time "alone" was precious and not to be wasted or spent sulking. Instead, this time was to be used to figure out who God wanted me to be. I had the opportunity to give him undistracted devotion and to allow him to show me who I am. He also wanted to teach me and show me how deep his love was for me. He wanted me to know that as much as I longed for a husband, my God longed for *me*. That thought offered me perspective on how much God yearns to be in relationship with his people.

About this same time, my sister and brother-in-law moved back to town with their two small children and a third on the way. They were very busy. Since I had Fridays off, I offered to help. Little did I know that what started out as me helping them would turn into them helping me. Time with my sister's family forever changed me. In serving them I found more purpose in my life than ever before. Witnessing their selfless, life-giving love on a daily basis helped me understand on a practical level what I had been reading and learning about. It also gave me an opportunity to see the face of God every time I looked at those sweet children. I was so drawn to the pure joy and fulfillment it gave me.

At different points in my journey, doubt crept in. Everyone told me that I was never going to meet a man at my sister's house. Sometimes I would try to seek the fulfillment of these desires out in the world again. Thankfully, the Lord continually brought me back to a place of contentment. He told me to surrender those desires into his hands.

A few guys came along who showed some interest, but I began these relationships by pursuing a friendship. A couple of them fled when I told them I was not going to have sex until I was married. With others, the mutual interest did not turn out to be anything more than initial attraction, and friendship remained.

After four years of living single, I talked three of my cousins into going on a young adult retreat with me. In my mind, it was a chance for cousin bonding and quality time with God. Going into the weekend, I swore off any distractions that might divert my focus. My cousins teased me on the drive over about being old and still single. Then one of them asserted, "I have a feeling you are going to meet your future husband this weekend." I brushed her off, explaining that I was not going to think about men this weekend. I planned to focus on God.

At the dreaded icebreaker that night, I was introduced to a handsome guy in the back of the room. I did not think much about it. Later that night, however, the same cousin who had spoken about marriage to me on the car trip over said, "That guy in the back of the room is going to be your husband." I laughed it off.

This declaration became one of many about *that guy* over the weekend. As the details unfolded, it turned out that the mutual friend who introduced us had had a vision of my face when she met him. She was surprised to see me when I arrived at the retreat and, inspired by the Holy Spirit, felt she *had* to introduce us.

My father, who was also at this event serving on the prayer team, pulled me aside to tell me he had met this guy a year before and had said to a friend, "For some reason, I feel like he is going to be my son-in-law." He also reminded me of a random phone call I received from a friend about two years prior, telling me he met the guy that I was supposed to marry! All the same guy—the handsome one from the back of the room.

At the end of the weekend, I learned that after this guy met me, he turned to the woman who introduced us (not knowing why she introduced us) and said, "I know this is weird, but I feel like she is going to be my future wife."

Hearing all of these remarkable accounts was overwhelming. So much for focusing only on Jesus that weekend. I was totally distracted. I finally worked up the courage to speak to him. I learned his name was Stephen. However, after talking with him, I was still not convinced he was *the one.*

I left the retreat uncertain where it would lead. *Besides,* I reasoned, *he never even asked for my phone number.* When I got home, I told my mom the entire story. With a huge grin on her face, she said that the night before, while speaking with her sister, she had predicted I was going to meet my future husband over the weekend. Now, this was just *crazy.* Was it even possible? Stephen and I lived three hours apart. Realistically, I would probably never even see him again.

At midnight that night, I received a text message from Stephen, saying he was glad we met and that he wanted to call me. He then said, "But I would like to wait nine days. I want to pray a novena [a nine-day prayer] before we talk to make sure to start off on the right foot." Those were nine long days, but on the ninth day, my phone rang. Thus began our two-and-a-half-year courtship.

I must have tipped the scales of doubt for God to go to the lengths he did to convince me he had a plan for me from the beginning. He was in control. He had orchestrated all of that just for me! He loved me so much that he created this elaborate plan just to show me his love and to give me the desires of my heart. I finally realized that I ravish my *Lord's* heart! How incredibly humbling.

Even though it was a fairy-tale meeting, our courtship was far from storybook. My future husband and I had only experienced relationship the wrong way. We had to relearn how to love and respect the other the way God intended, not just in theory but also in practice.

We had to make a conscious effort to stay in prayer both individually and collectively for our chastity. We had to seek frequent counsel and accountability. Anytime we let our guard down, the enemy pounced. We would experience the joy turn into guilt and shame, motivating us back to the confessional.

We also had to learn how to communicate and show our love for each other in nonsexual ways. Once we understood the truth about the sacredness and beauty of sex, we desired to wait for the fullness of married love. It took effort, patience, perseverance, and a great deal of prayer, but God's grace gave us the strength. On April 2, 2009 (two days before my thirtieth birthday), Stephen brought me back to the church where we met for the conference. As we knelt in prayer in the chapel, he proposed to me. On January 1, 2010, in front of God and all our devoted community, we became *one* in the Sacrament of Holy Matrimony. The emotions of that day are indescribable. I walked into church and there was my Prince Charming standing at the front, waiting for *me*. The man I had prayed for long before we met. The man who loved me and respected me enough to wait until this day to express fully his love. The man handpicked by God and the fulfillment of my desire.

Stephen's look said it all: *You have ravished my heart, my sister, my bride.* I finally felt like the cherished and adored beauty worth fighting for. I couldn't wait to love him for the rest of my life! That night he carried me over the threshold to a room lit with candles, rose petals on the floor forming a path to a Bible, opened to the book of Tobit. We prayed this together: "'Now, not with lust, but with fidelity I take this kinswoman as my wife. Send down your mercy on me and on her, and grant that we may grow old together. . . .' They said together, 'Amen, amen!'" (8:7–8).

In our communion, together with our God, I felt exceedingly more joy and fulfillment than anything the world has ever offered me. The gratitude for what the Lord has done for me continues to ravage my heart.

# Take a Moment

1. Pray with the following scripture from Tobit 8:5–8:

> "Blessed are you, O God of our ancestors;
>   blessed be your name forever and ever!
> Let the heavens and all your creation bless you forever.
> You made Adam, and you made his wife Eve
>   to be his helper and support;
>   and from these two the human race has come.
> You said, 'It is not good for the man to be alone;
>   let us make him a helper like himself.'
> Now, not with lust,
>   but with fidelity I take this kinswoman as my wife.
> Send down your mercy on me and on her,
>   and grant that we may grow old together.
> Bless us with children."
>
> They said together, "Amen, amen!"

   a. Read the scripture passage once and become familiar with the text.
   b. Slowly read the passage a second time.
   c. Very, very slowly read the passage a third time, paying attention to the words and phrases that rest in your heart. What is God speaking to you through this passage?

2. The Lord wants to be invited into *every* part of our lives. What comes up in your heart when you imagine inviting his Spirit into your intimate encounters, as Tobias did in the verse above? Is it peace, or shame? If you are unable to imagine it, ask the

Holy Spirit to help you see why not, and to reveal any areas of distorted love and lust.

3.  Ask your divine Bridegroom to purify your own desires, and to show you the truth of authentic love—both his love for you, and how he desires you to be loved by a man. What is he speaking to your heart in this place?

# Never Alone

## LISA BRENNINKMEYER

It's amazing what you can pack down deep in the soul and ignore for decades. A knot can form within the heart, but it's possible to bury it and disregard its importance. Busyness can keep introspection at bay. Achievements try to convince you that self-reflection isn't necessary. But when a crisis hits, it all starts to unravel at an alarming pace. When this happened to me, I remember wanting more than anything to shove everything back in Pandora's box and sit on the lid. Binge-watching Netflix with a glass of wine or two promised to help me numb out. But I discovered something that gave me the courage to lift the lid and look at my heart. You can't selectively numb emotions. If I numbed the scary, dark, and overwhelming, I ended up numbing the joy too. The result? It started to feel like events were just washing over me. I realized that I just might miss living my one wild and beautiful life.

Author Danielle LaPorte asks, "Can you remember who you were before the world told you who you should be?"[1] Her question challenged me to go back in order to move forward, and it gave me permission to reflect on a time when my heart felt free. It made me think about my childhood and how rooted I was in my true identity. I had the rare gift of being raised in a family that taught me that I was unconditionally loved by God, and that nothing I could do could make him love me more or less. I knew I was his beloved daughter, and for the most part I lived out of that identity. Were there childhood hurts and dashed dreams? Of course; no one floats through childhood and adolescence without some bumps. But by and large, I could return to my solid foundation and remember who I was.

Have you ever noticed how some of our character traits and behaviors can earn us accolades, but when we analyze things a bit, we realize that they've led to some self-destructive behavior? For me, being able to sense people's needs and emotions and adapt accordingly is a skill that has been something of a double-edged sword. While I'm grateful that I can often trust my gut, I sometimes wish that I was blissfully unaware of what other people are feeling. Picking up on others' cues has all too often led me to unbalanced people pleasing. Valuing harmony above all in relationships has frequently caused me to sacrifice who I am in order to be who someone else needed me to be.

But those sacrifices can pay off in the short term. I put those skills to use when I first got married and moved to Germany. Adjusting to a new culture, learning a language, and being a good wife to Leo meant that adaptation and change were survival skills I couldn't do without. My husband was running his own race—trying to prove his worth in a family business where the bar was set high. We both desperately needed the other to be the safe place to land, but lacking the words to ask for it, we ended up unintentionally pushing each other to perform.

My life as a new bride felt like the school of hard knocks. It seemed that the only way I could learn how to behave, dress, and speak was by making a mistake, feeling the heat of disapproval, and resolving to get it right next time. But no matter how many adjustments I made, I couldn't seem to get it right—which, for me, meant doing it all perfectly.

Early on in our marriage, I went away for the weekend with the wives of Leo's colleagues. In my mind, it was critical that they liked me. Leo's work was the bedrock of our social life. Everything was intertwined, and failure in one area seemed to affect all others. At this particular gathering, I was determined to make friends. Three months pregnant and fighting nausea, I spent hours on the edges of the social circles. I had started to learn German, but the only way I could keep up with conversation was by watching facial expressions and mirroring them. Exhausted by the efforts, I finally sat down in a chair and analyzed my appearance. My clothes were too bright. My bangs were too long. My purse wasn't the right brand. Everything felt wrong, and the loneliness was overwhelming.

As I sat there listening to the dull murmur of German words, I picked up on an English conversation taking place behind me. It seemed strange to me that they'd all be talking in English since it wasn't their mother tongue. Then I realized that they were talking about me, and speaking in English precisely so that I would hear. It seemed that my wedding stationery had caused confusion. In Germany, it's conventional to hyphenate your married name and your maiden name. One reason for this is to let people know where you come from. That seemed to be the problem. No one could figure out who my people were, and it was very clear that they doubted my pedigree was up to snuff. At first I ignored the conversation, but finally I mustered up the little bit of courage I had (which wasn't very much) and walked over to the group. "Excuse me," I said. "You seem to be having trouble figuring out who I am, so I thought I'd say hi and explain. If I'd written out my new name the way you are suggesting, I would have felt like I was making some kind of a feminist statement—like Leo's name wasn't enough. His name is enough for me. But my maiden name is Harris, in case you want to check me out." And then I marched to the bathroom, where I promptly threw up.

I ran back to the house where I was staying, a place I would return to many times during my years in Germany. The home was run by a housekeeper who I thought would offer me comfort. She was one of the few people who spoke English to me. But when I burst into tears the minute I walked through the door, she grabbed me roughly by the arm and sat me down in the living room. "Do you not know who you are?" she asked. "You are now Frau Brenninkmeyer, and you will learn to act like her." And so the tutorials began. She taught me how to speak, dress, and act, and what kind of Christmas cards to send. It seemed like she was helping me. But in reality I was being offered a counterfeit identity—one tied to my accomplishments and reputation. What seemed like my ticket to acceptance and freedom was actually leading me to a place of bondage.

I grew increasingly miserable, and I finally sat Leo down to tell him how unhappy I was. I poured out my heart, and he looked both uncomfortable and irritated. "Do you expect me to quit my job?" he asked. "I didn't ask you to make any of these sacrifices, and I'm not going to spend the rest of my life trying to make it all up to you. This is what you chose." What I didn't know then but realize now was how incredibly hard he was trying to make life work, to be enough, to survive. All I heard was the fact that he was not going to be my knight in shining armor. He was not going to charge in and make it all better. And in that moment, the enemy of my soul began to whisper the most destructive of lies: *You're all alone. No one is going to come and help you. It isn't safe to trust. It's all up to you.*

Those lies made so much sense to me. They felt true. And the truth that I had grown up believing faded into the background. Agreeing with those lies made me feel vulnerable and afraid, so I made a vow: *I will never need him.* I spent the next two decades of my life living out that vow. Grabbing hold of a counterfeit identity, I began to achieve in order to prove my worth. Placing my security in my accomplishments led me to a place of self-reliance that sabotaged one of my deepest desires, to be a loving wife. My self-protection got in the way of receiving Leo's love, and I walled off the tender part within me that required vulnerability. I served and loved Leo and created a beautiful home. But what he wanted most was the real me, and I kept her hidden within.

Fast-forward twenty years. I was in the midst of my worst nightmare. I had prayed that my children would be emotionally healthy and protected from family dysfunction. My greatest desire was to lead them to a life-giving relationship with the Lord, and I could see the fruit of those efforts. I had been doing the right things. My children had been doing the right things. Yet somehow, depression and despair had seeped into the heart of my precious son. He was in a place of such emotional darkness that I couldn't reach him. Fear paralyzed me. All my emotions began to unravel, and my coping mechanism of performing and achieving did not help me. There was simply nothing I could do but pray. I found myself wandering from room to room in my house for hours at a time.

This paralysis led me to a counselor who helped me journey backward in order to move forward. Although I went to her for my son, she was also concerned about me. After a few sessions, she commented on the fact that I was guarded. I was initially taken aback by her words, because I considered myself to be transparent. I gave talks and wrote Bible studies and bared my soul. There was very little I wasn't willing to share if I thought it would help another woman draw closer to Christ. So how could she say I was guarded? But the more she probed, the more I came to see that I choose very carefully who I am honest with, and much of the time, I keep the most vulnerable part of my heart out of sight. I explained to her that not very many people felt safe to me. So I curated my words and gave people just enough of me for them to think that I'd shared my heart, but kept the core of my truth to myself.

The counselor asked if I behaved this way with the people closest to me. I thought about it for a moment. "I think I am more guarded with those I love than with strangers," I said. She asked if they knew how careful I was—how much I kept hidden. "Of course not," I replied. "I'm pretty good at this."

Then she spoke words that pierced me with a severe mercy. She explained that it was impossible to self-protect and love at the same time. With those words she disabled one of my self-protection tools forever. My heart was becoming undone, Pandora's box was looking really appealing, and Leo was coming home from a business trip. I was a mess, and I knew he'd want to know why. More than anything, I wanted to make something up and be left alone—to numb out. But my desire to love well was stronger than my desire to self-protect. So I begged God to give me just a little more courage than fear to help me to be honest.

Leo came home and knew something was wrong. We sat down, and he asked what was going on. By God's grace, I was honest and let my heart and words unravel. I started with a confession, asking his forgiveness for defining him in my heart by one conversation, decades ago. I asked him to forgive me for my vow—for my refusal to need him—for my determination to rely on no one but myself. I asked him to accompany me as my heart continued to unravel. I knew that there was more soul work to be done and that it might get messy. We returned to that conversation in Germany, twenty years earlier, and walked through it again. He asked my forgiveness. We gave grace to each other, and began to learn to dance again.

The darkness around our son didn't go away for quite some time. We battled it together, and scripture and prayer proved to be the greatest weapons. But God, in his faithfulness, fought for all our hearts. The Lion of Judah never took his eyes off of us and never left our sides.

In the moments of hurt and crisis, it seemed as if I was alone. This was the lie the enemy whispered to my son, too. We both doubted that anyone was going to come through for us, and we fell hard into the trap of self-reliance. We both reached a point where there was nowhere else to turn. Our best efforts could not lift us out of our circumstances. We were broken and overcome with weakness. And it was there that God did his deepest and most significant work of healing.

St. Augustine said, "I saw His glory in my wounds, and it dazzled me."[2] This is what happened to us. In our place of woundedness and weakness, God showed up and gave us a vision of himself that changed everything. It wasn't a flashing vision but a deep awareness of his presence and a belief that he has *always* been there. In that moment in Germany when I was offered a counterfeit identity, he was there calling me his beloved, chosen daughter. Each time that I self-protected and hid my true self, he was there ready to be my shield. When my son was slipping into the darkness, the Lord grabbed his hand and never lost his grip. When it felt like there was an ocean of distance between my heart and my husband's, God grabbed hold of both and drew them together. Always there. Always present. Never leaving me alone.

## Take a Moment

1. Pray with the following scripture from Romans 8:14–17:

   > For those who are led by the Spirit of God are children of God. For you did not receive a spirit of slavery to fall back into fear, but you received a spirit of adoption, through which we cry, "Abba, Father!" The Spirit itself bears witness with our spirit that we are children of God, and if children, then heirs, heirs of God and joint heirs with Christ, if only we suffer with him so that we may also be glorified with him.

   a. Read the scripture passage once and become familiar with the text.
   b. Slowly read the passage a second time.
   c. Very, very slowly read the passage a third time, paying attention to the words and phrases that rest in your heart. What is God speaking to you through this passage?

2. How does coming to know your identity as a beloved daughter affect your identity as bride?

3. Journal about a time in your life when God the Father brought something good out of intense personal pain, creating meaning out of suffering that felt wasted previously.

# The Fulfillment of All Desire

## JEN SETTLE

Like many little girls, I grew up dreaming of becoming a wife and a mother. I played house and fed my baby dolls until their imaginary tummies were happy and full. All I ever wanted was a real family of my own. As the youngest of nine children, I developed an understanding that what we *do* in our family is grow up, go to college, date, get married, and have kids. That was what everyone did. Naturally, I assumed I'd go to college, find Mr. Right, get married, have children, and live happily ever after.

When I left home for college, I was in search of *the one*. After four years with no prospects, panic set in. *Why wasn't God helping me find my husband?* He wanted me to be happy, right? Doubts, fears, and insecurities began to overwhelm me. *What is wrong with me? Why doesn't any guy want to marry me?*

After college, I told myself that my timing would just be different from everyone else's in my family. I moved to a new city and found an amazing Catholic community of young adults that became like family to me. Together we grew in our faith and helped one another discern our vocations—although I remember specifically thinking, *Discern? What's there to discern? I already know my vocation.*

My friends understood my ache for marriage because they, too, were experiencing that same longing. Sometimes I was content with waiting on God's timing. Other times my ache turned to grasping. I remember going to daily Mass and watching single guys come in, thinking, *Is that him? Is he going to be my husband?* I looked at every man I met as the potential *one.*

Eventually my friends began to get married and have children, and although I was genuinely happy for them, it only made the ache swell. I resented God for giving me a desire he wasn't fulfilling.

Even with the resentment, I remained faithful to my relationship with God. I desired him deeply. I sought him in prayer, adoration, and the sacraments. I worked for the Church, teaching theology and directing others to teach in our parish programs. As fulfilling as all of that was, it couldn't fill the longing in my heart to live my vocation of marriage and family. When I began to lose hope, I was introduced to St. John Paul II's theology of the body.[1]

The moment I heard my first talk, I knew God was speaking to me. He was speaking to the depth of who I was—who I was created to be. I learned that my desire for spousal love and motherhood was something God had created in me, as a woman, and that he had every intention of fulfilling it. Coming to this knowledge brought hope back into my heart.

I remember the first time I heard the phrase *spousal meaning of the body.* I immediately thought, *Well, that is something I'll eventually live when I get married.* "Spousal meaning of the body" actually refers to love in which a human person "becomes a gift and—through this gift—fulfills the very meaning of his being and existence" (*TOB* 15:1). What was the spousal meaning of *my* body, if I wasn't married and didn't have children? How could my body be spousal?

I took this question to my holy hour. *How do I express love in my singleness, Lord? How am I a gift in my singleness?* As I opened my heart to him, examples of my life came beautifully into focus. I can give more time and attention to those whom I love and serve because of my singleness. Every time I give the gift of myself in love, I fulfill all for which I was created—to love and to bring forth life from that love.

After this experience in prayer, I began to see things differently. I came to understand that my ultimate spouse is *Christ*. He is the Bridegroom, and each of us, as a member of the Church, is meant to be his bride for all eternity. I experience the spousal meaning of my body every time I offer my time, my heart, my prayer, my service, myself, to someone else. Ultimately I am offering it to my spouse—Christ. From that offering, from the gift that I am to him and he is to me, life is brought forth through *our* love.

With expectant hope, I began to understand my call to spiritual motherhood. This call led me to mother many spiritual children, experiencing the depth of a mother's love for her children. It was then that I understood what St. Paul meant when he wrote in his letter to the Galatians: "Rejoice, you childless one, you who bear no children, burst into song and shout, you who endure no birth pangs; for the children of the desolate woman are more numerous than the children of the one who is married" (Gal 4:27, NRSV). The Lord was quietly showing me the ways that I previously had not been living my singleness as a gift.

He also revealed to me that in those times that I was grasping for a spouse, seeking a man to fulfill my ache, I hadn't truly seen each man before me for who he was. I missed knowing and being a part of the lives of these men, as their sister and friend. Paradoxically, when I was at Mass looking for a spouse, he *was* there all along—in the Eucharist!

The Lord gently revealed that I had made an idol of marriage. There was genuineness to my desire to love another, but I placed finding an earthly spousal love above loving my heavenly spouse. I was too attached to my own desires and not open to God's good desires *for me*. I was never open to the idea that he might have a desire for me to live out the spousal meaning of my body in another way.

He was leading me down a path of purification of my desires. I had to be honest with myself and God about how much I idolized marriage and family. I had to talk with him about how much I didn't trust in his plan for me. I had to seek forgiveness for all of the things I had placed above him. It was in the surrender that I found joy.

As I came to experience peace in my singleness, the Lord showed me his desire for me to be an exclusive gift to him. He opened my heart to live out my feminine call to spousal love and motherhood through the vocation of consecrated virginity. I had no idea the desire to be a spouse and a mother would be fulfilled through a religious vocation. If you had told me even a year before that I would be receptive to the idea of living the religious life, I would not have believed it. Then I read of the charism of this vocation that spoke deeply to my heart: *To be a bride of Christ and to live spiritual motherhood and intercessory prayer for priests, seminarians, and laypeople.*

As I made the journey through discernment of this vocation, I felt the Lord's guiding hand. An essential step on this journey was a retreat with my spiritual director. Neither of us knew what the theme of the retreat would be, but on our first day, my spiritual director said that he felt the Lord asking him to guide me on a path of greater clarity. Father said, "You need to grieve marriage and family." I immediately responded, "Father, I've already done that, so it must be something else." As only a longtime spiritual director can do, he looked at me with great love, but also confidence that he knew what the Lord was asking.

As his spiritual daughter, I trusted his guidance. He asked me to spend the whole day writing a bullet-point outline of my call to consecrated life. I needed to be rooted and grounded in the truth of my call before entering into the process of letting go of the desire for earthly marriage and family. That day was filled with so much joy. As I sat in the chapel reflecting, I felt so confident, so secure in knowing God's desire for me and my desire for him.

When I met with my director the following day, he said, "I want you to spend today writing a bullet-point list of all of the things you will not experience in marriage and family. List the desires of your heart, no matter how insignificant they seem. Leave nothing out." I sat before the Lord and spilled my heart open—from the obvious points of not experiencing the one-flesh union with my husband and the children that would follow, to the less obvious desires of my heart to pick out a wedding dress and walk down the aisle toward my future spouse. Then the desire to have a husband give me roses and tell me he loves me . . . my journal became a very long list of seemingly unfulfilled longings and desires.

When I met with my spiritual director the next day, he asked me to go back to each of the points in my journal and speak with the Lord about how not experiencing them makes me feel. He asked me to open my heart. "Leave no stone unturned. Leave no feeling left unspoken to him. Know that you are loved and that he wants to hear every part of your heart." So that day became a day of unveiling. I spoke to the Lord about how each of those unfulfilled desires of my heart made me feel. I was sad, angry, and disappointed. I let him love me in those places of disappointment and unfulfilled desires. With the sharing of each point, I could feel myself giving him more of my heart until I felt I had no more disappointments or desires left to give him.

On this final day of my retreat, my director said, "Now I want you to go back through the list one more time and let the Lord speak to you about each of the desires of your heart for marriage and family. Just be with him. Don't speak. Allow him to speak. Listen to his heart and his desires for you." As I opened my journal, the Lord poured out his heart to me and I was reading his words as they appeared on the pages. He spoke to me about how he not only desires to fulfill the longings of my heart for marriage and family, but that he will. "Each and every time you receive me in the Eucharist, we become one. Many spiritual children will be born from our spousal love. You *are* a mother, and your motherly heart will only expand with more love for more children."

My heart felt so much joy and lightness. It opened to receive the Lord and his desires for me, but I still had one lingering question: "What about the little desires, Lord? Do you want to fulfill those too?" As I spoke those words, my attention was diverted; I noticed for the first time that two dozen roses were placed on each side of the tabernacle. *Why hadn't I noticed those before? It's Lent. There aren't supposed to be flowers in the chapel.* As I finished that thought, I went back to my journal and what came forth was, "My dearest Jen, those roses are for you, from me. I love you." All I could do was smile.

After the retreat, I stopped discerning my vocation and entered deeply into formation. A year later, I walked down the aisle of the basilica in my wedding gown. In the sanctuary, as in all the daily Masses I had attended searching for my bridegroom, he was there, waiting for me. On the feast of the Presentation of Jesus, I presented myself to him, and the Church, as his bride. Just as Our Lady and St. Joseph presented the gift of Jesus to the Lord in the Temple, I presented the gift of myself to Jesus. He received the gift of my feminine, bridal heart, and he gave the gift of himself to me in the Eucharist. This was the fulfillment I had ached and longed for throughout my single life. Jesus is the fulfillment of all my desires.

## Take a Moment

1. Pray with the following passage from St. John Paul II's *Theology of the Body* 15:1:

   The spousal meaning of the body refers to the body's power to express love: precisely that love in which a human person becomes a gift and—through this gift—fulfills the very meaning of his being and existence.

    a.   Read the passage once and become familiar with the text.

    b.   Slowly read the passage a second time.

    c.   Very, very slowly read the passage a third time, paying attention to the words and phrases that rest in your heart. What is God speaking to you through this passage?

2.  What stirs in your heart when you hear you are created for relationship with Jesus as Bridegroom?

3.  Are you a gift in the way you offer yourself in relationship? Why or why not?

# Love Reclaimed

## JEANNIE HANNEMANN

It all began when my husband found his father's pornography. Those images gripped his tender spirit. Pornography became his secret obsession. He disclosed his problem to me before marriage, but we both naively thought once we were married and could be intimate, he would have no desire for pornography. We were wrong! While we were still newlyweds, I discovered a *Playboy* magazine in our home. My stomach tightened into a knot, my heart began racing, and I angrily confronted him. He apologized and said he wouldn't use pornography again. I wanted to trust him but was frightened. The knot in my stomach was my constant companion.

I knew my husband was sincere about quitting, but eventually his willpower would wane. Each time he gave in to lust, the knot in my stomach grew tighter. At one point, I threatened divorce, he went into treatment, and I believed things were better. The truth was he wasn't better at staying away from sexual sin, just better at keeping it a secret. Unbeknownst to me, when internet pornography became available, he spiraled out of control. The day he broke down and confessed he was a porn addict, my world shattered. I could hardly believe the terrible things my husband was saying. The man I loved so completely was telling me about his decades-long deception, lies, and immorality. As he elaborated on his secret sexual life, I became dizzy, my palms began sweating, I sobbed hysterically, and the knot in my stomach constricted so much that

81

I had trouble breathing! I now know that the knot has a name—betrayal trauma.

To feel unsafe and insecure in my most important relationship crippled me. I couldn't sleep, eat, or carry on a conversation. My fears made me hypervigilant, and my imagination vividly portrayed worst-case scenarios. My husband's disclosure of sexual sins made me feel vulnerable and violated. During that time of angst, I felt as though every betrayal in my life was being unveiled and was brutally annihilating me. Self-doubt immersed me, and I focused on guarding his every action to protect myself from more agony.

I was tempted, tested, and tried in my confused state. Should I divorce him? Should I tell others? Should I keep it a secret? I had so many questions. I felt ashamed and worried about what others would think of my husband and me if they found out. How would our adult children handle this news? The few people I had confided in didn't know what to say. One friend told me my husband might not look elsewhere if I lost weight and dressed nicer. This reinforced my thinking that there must be something terribly wrong with me if my husband preferred masturbating to pornography over having sex with me. I had believed our infrequent sexual bonding was because he had a low sex drive. Now I was faced with the thought that he just didn't want me.

Facing the devastation of my husband's pornography addiction left me physically fatigued, emotionally exhausted, mentally confused, and spiritually terrified. The trauma from being betrayed was intense and immense. Everything I believed about my life had been destroyed, especially my self-worth. I was further traumatized when I went looking for professional support. Therapists minimized his actions, and clergy blamed me for his acting out. Eventually I found the support I needed in a book by another betrayed wife. As I read her story, I saw my own. For the first time since the nightmare began, I didn't feel so alone. It might have been just print on a page, but to me it was a soul sister who offered comfort.

At about this time, my mother was diagnosed with ovarian cancer. Chemotherapy was administered in a room with a dozen women hooked up to the medicine that brought hope for healing but caused so much suffering in the process. Caregivers sat in chairs next to their loved ones and read books. Out of respect for the sick patients, no one talked to one another. Even the nurses used hushed voices. One day I sat by my mother reading the book written by the betrayed wife. A hospital volunteer passing out cookies broke the silence and asked me what I was reading. I was so shocked that I blurted out, "*An Affair of the Mind,* a book for women whose husbands use pornography."[1] She dropped the plate of cookies and ran out of the room. A nurse quickly came over and asked me what had happened. When I told her, she said, "I need that book." A young wife who was hooked up to chemotherapy next to my mother began crying and asked me for the title of the book and said, "I need it too." As I looked around the room, several other women were crying and whispering, "I need it too." Within seconds, we were no longer isolated individuals; we were a community of women not just fighting cancer but also another silent killer: pornography. It was a grace-filled moment of transformation for me. I stopped focusing on feeling sorry for myself or worrying about my husband's behavior. I recognized the work of Satan. God's plan was to have no sickness or death and for husbands to protect their wives. I saw the pain in that room and knew the source was the evil one who wanted to destroy humanity. I stopped seeing my husband as the enemy. I knew we had to stop fighting each other and begin combatting the real enemy together.

I called to confide in an out-of-town friend who was a great prayer warrior. Her reaction was swift and serious. She told me it was time to honor my marriage vows and give witness to them. (I must admit my first reaction was to be hurt that she didn't feel sorry for me!) She challenged me to action. Later she called with names of therapists and clergy who were ready to help. She became a loving confidante as I dealt with the effects of betrayal trauma, but she

never let me feel sorry for myself again. Her constant reminder of
the availability of God's grace motivated me to trust in the powerful
scripture passage of Romans 8:28 that says God will bring good out
of every situation.

By God's grace, we found an online recovery program designed
to heal brain damage caused by internet porn that destroys the
ability to think and follow moral reasoning. My husband also
began working with a spiritual director who was well versed in
the problem, and his new therapist held him accountable. He went
to regular Confession and even saw an exorcist. I watched with
a grateful heart as these support efforts eventually led him to a
powerful healing of body, mind, and spirit. But it seemed as he
ascended from the darkness, I sank deeper into despair. This made
no sense to me. I should be happy that he had regained his ability
to function in society and be free from sexual sins. Where I should
have had hope, I felt more despondency. I realized my own recovery
had been buried as we were absorbed in seeking treatment for him.

As I searched for personal help, I discovered more women in
my situation. We were all Catholics looking for real solutions. We
met weekly to help each other navigate the maze of betrayal trauma.
After many tearful conversations, we began to feel safe enough to
give voice to our own buried truths. Each of us said it in different
ways, but we were all crying out with a loss of self-respect and
destroyed dignity. Many of us blamed ourselves and thought we
weren't good enough to keep our husbands happy.

One day while praying the Rosary, I thought of how Mary was
also gripped with fear when she heard God's plan for her life. We
know this because the angel Gabriel tells her not to be afraid. Then
he gives her the most amazing gift. He tells her about Elizabeth,
another woman experiencing an unusual pregnancy, and proclaims
that nothing is impossible with God.

I realized that the way to healing from my husband's betrayal
was to find an Elizabeth, a woman who would understand my pain
and show me nothing is impossible with God. Just as quickly as I

had that thought, the name of an older woman crossed my mind. She had confided in me years ago that her husband had an affair. She had remained married to him and always seemed filled with joy. I went to see her and poured out my heart to this woman. As she embraced me, I felt safe for the first time since my husband's disclosure. She lovingly looked in my eyes and said, "Honey, you are looking for your self-worth to come from your husband's loving behavior. Your dignity comes from God alone. Once you realize that, nothing your husband does or doesn't do can destroy you! My joy comes in knowing I am the beloved daughter of God." She offered me encouragement to keep fighting for my marriage and to trust in God to sustain me.

I went to the eucharistic adoration chapel to ponder the things she shared. In the chapel was a statue of Mary. I begged Mary to help me overcome my fear. I had planned to stay an hour but ended up spending the entire night. After many tears, my body and mind became quiet, and for the first time in a long time, I just listened. Slowly, thoughts and images began seeping into my mind that showed me quite clearly that I had made my husband the center of my life. My husband had committed adultery, but I had succumbed to idolatry. I had given my husband the role that belongs to God alone. God needed to be the center of my life. I had been so busy pointing out my husband's sins that I did not recognize the ones I had committed. I had allowed the demands and attractions of life to gain my attention and devotion. I saw that my husband's recovery had become more important to me than my relationship with God. Once I recognized these personal transgressions, I felt Mary take me by the hand and lead me back to her Son. She showed me he understood betrayal trauma. Images of the garden of Gethsemane, Judas's kiss of betrayal, and the rooster crowing filled my mind. The loneliness I had been feeling left me. I knew beyond a doubt that my God understood my pain and would heal me.

God also showed me I had abandonment issues from childhood that were compounding the betrayal from my husband. Slowly the

lies that had tied up that first betrayal knot in my childhood were
being undone. I recognized the weaknesses and limitations in my
parents' lives, and the hurt that I didn't even realize I had carried for
my entire life vanished and that knot in my stomach was loosened.
I saw lies from my youth about the importance of my appearance,
grades, and social status that had cinched that betrayal knot so
many times. My insecurities now made sense to me, and I understood that my husband's adultery had triggered all my past traumas.
God then persuaded me to see that my worth is not based on how
I look, on who I know, on my work, or even on my relationships as
wife and mother. The truth finally reached the essence of my being
that God's love is what makes me valuable. He created me and has
wonderful plans for my life. He wants to heal my wounds and bring
me to peace and joy.

I left the eucharistic adoration chapel just as the sun was rising. I immediately recalled the words in Zechariah's canticle: "In
the tender compassion of our Lord, the dawn from on high shall
break upon us, to shine on those who dwell in darkness and the
shadow of death, and to guide our feet into the way of peace" (see
Lk 1:78–79). I was moving into the light in more ways than one.

It is amazing to live in the awareness that God has always loved
me, even when others failed to do so, and to know it is enough!
When I confessed my idolatry in the Sacrament of Reconciliation, I
was blessed with the grace to join my husband in a restored life. We
reclaimed God's plan for our lives, and today our spirits join Mary
as we rejoice in God our Savior! We now operate a ministry to help
men and women who suffer from, or are affected by, unhealthy sexual behaviors. We have walked with thousands of men and women
who have discovered the same healing by God's grace.

My betrayal knot was completely undone one early Christmas morning, when a couple my husband and I mentored out of
divorce invited me to be present at the birth of their baby. As the
baby cried out, all my betrayal tears were sanctified as I witnessed

1 John 4:18: "Perfect love drives out fear." God brought good out of our suffering. I now know that goodness has a name: Eternal Love.

## Take a Moment

1.  Pray with the following scripture passage from 1 John 4:18:

    > There is no fear in love, but perfect love drives out fear
    > because fear has to do with punishment, and so one who
    > fears is not yet perfect in love.

    a.  Read the scripture passage once and become familiar with the text.
    b.  Slowly read the passage a second time.
    c.  Very, very slowly read the passage a third time, paying attention to the words and phrases that rest in your heart. What is God speaking to you through this passage?
2.  Have you ever felt betrayal from a husband or boyfriend? Are you aware of feelings of fear and powerlessness in relation to that broken trust?
3.  Do you believe fear is from God? What barriers prevent you from receiving his perfect love?

# Inner Healing Prayer

## BRIDE IDENTITY

## BOB SCHUCHTS

As you engage in this meditative and contemplative prayer experience, allow the Holy Spirit to lead you. Pause after each step to record your experiences in a journal.

1. Ask the Holy Spirit to show you the specific and general ways you have received love and nurturing as a bride (with a husband or with Jesus). Record these reflections in your journal and write a prayer of thanksgiving for these gifts of love and nurture.

2. Ask the Holy Spirit to reveal to you how and when you were wounded in your identity as bride—in dating, courtship, marriage, divorce, or by becoming a widow. You may have memories, feelings, or thoughts about not being loved, desired, or fought for. Let yourself experience what it has been like to be wounded as a bride. Record what you experience in your journal.

3.  Ask the Holy Spirit to reveal to you the knots that have kept your heart from living freely, fully, faithfully, and fruitfully as a bride. What are the lies underlying these knots? Write down the knots and the lies in your journal.

4.  Ask the Holy Spirit to allow you to experience being the bride of Christ in a very personal way. Through meditation and contemplation, experience his chaste and holy love. Receive his tender and faithful love as a healing of any wounds you have experienced. In your sanctified imagination, watch how he relates to you and listen to what he says to you. Write in your prayer journal what you saw, thought, felt, and desired.

5.  Ask the Holy Spirit to reveal to you the truth about your identity as bride in any areas where the lies took root in your heart. Record these truths in your journal.

6.  Finally, ask Mary, the perfected image of bride, to show you how to untie the knots that were formed in your relationships with men. Come back in a few weeks and record how things have changed regarding these knots.

7.  Close with a prayer of thanksgiving to Jesus for loving you freely, fully, faithfully, and fruitfully as his bride.

# PART IV

## Mother

## BOB SCHUCHTS

Whether you have biological or spiritual children, you are called to be a mother. Our Blessed Mother, Mary, is the model for all mothers. By God's design, mothers are meant to be open to life; to love their children unconditionally; and to nurture, protect, teach, guide, and bless their children. In return, children respond with love, honor, and obedience. Has this been your experience?

In this part, Nicole, Debra, Barbra, and Carrie share their personal reflections on what it has been like being a mother. As you read their stories, I encourage you to think about your own experience of being a mother. At the end of this part, you will have an opportunity to bring to prayer all you have experienced as a mother—as a way of receiving a deeper blessing and healing in your authentic identity as beloved mother.

# Extraordinary Love

## NICOLE RODRIGUEZ

Have you ever noticed that God likes to work outside of our paradigm? He loves to do the unthinkable and the unimaginable in our lives. With the most ordinary of circumstances, he creates the extraordinary. Such as with the simple question posed to me many years ago: "How many children do you want?"

My story begins with a desire to have children in the beautifully ordinary way. After losing our first child to miscarriage, my husband, Lance, and I waited six long years before discovering with delight that I was pregnant again. Our excitement and joy for Thomas, our second baby boy, were understandably tempered with anxiety, and within just a few short weeks, our hopes were dashed.

We were both heartbroken. Instead of turning inward in our suffering, we made a choice to turn to God and our prayer community. As our community gathered around us to share in our suffering and to pray with us, one friend asked what seemed like an odd question under the circumstances: "How many children do you desire?" As faithful Catholics, we looked at each other and responded, "However many he wants to give, of course." Our friend continued, "God is saying you can have as many children as you want."

Another friend chimed in, "I have an image of many children and they just keep coming." We felt a mixture of excitement, encouragement, and complete bewilderment, all at the same time. How could this happen? These words of hope, supposedly from the Lord, didn't make sense to us at all. We were already in our midthirties, and my biological clock was ticking rapidly. Time was running out.

It would take us a long time to understand what the vision of many children meant and how God would fulfill this promise. The journey began with deep sadness and an unexpected invitation into Jesus' own passion. I vividly remember, during the night of my miscarriage with Thomas, an image flashing through my mind of Jesus being scourged, then carrying his Cross. I knew in this moment he was with me in my physical and emotional pain of loss. Carrying the Cross and looking intently at me, he said, "I had Thomas in mind; this was for him." I was struck by the great love in Jesus' eyes, and I knew it was love that drove him to the Cross—not just love for me but the reality of his love for this life I carried within my womb for only a few months. Jesus bore his suffering so that Thomas could dwell in glory with him. I realized that this life in my womb mattered—not only to me but also to the Savior of the universe!

Oh, how my heart ached with longing to hold my baby, to hold close this part of Lance and me. As I struggled forward in the following days, I distinctly understood that God was inviting me to enter into the pain of this moment rather than repress it. I encountered the knot of fear looking right at me. All I could do was be in my tears, in my pain, right where I was. This confrontation with the pain began to undo a huge knot of fear in my heart.

I recall sitting on my couch, weeping with grief for the loss of Thomas, when I heard the gentle voice of Jesus within my heart: "This is what it means to be human—to feel all your emotions is to be fully alive." With those words, a veil was lifted, exposing the depth of my ache and reconnecting me to the vulnerability of my little-girl heart. The utter abandonment I felt in that moment took my breath away. A new and deeper memory had cracked open, a deeper knot of abandonment that needed to be tenderly undone.

I was suddenly and simultaneously in touch with my heart as a child and as an adult grieving for the loss of my family. Just months after I was baptized into the Catholic Church at the age of eleven, my parents decided to divorce. Memories came flooding forth of how alone and abandoned I felt as a little girl. I saw images of myself yearning for my parents to be together and crying myself to sleep. The ache to belong to a family consumed me. As the memories played through my mind, I understood that not one of those moments was insignificant to Jesus.

As I began to connect to my foundational desire for family life and the deep wounds of my vulnerable little-girl heart, I recognized a hidden knot in my heart that distorted my understanding of my fundamental identity and had driven so many negative choices in my life. The painful wound of lost familial love had been caused by the lie that *I was alone* and *I was abandoned in the moments when I was most in need.* The Lord was patiently helping me embrace the reality that I am not abandoned in my suffering. He is closer than ever.

Worship music was very powerful during my grieving process. As tears filled my eyes and rolled down my cheeks, I could clearly feel in my heart the Father's love for me in the midst of my sorrow. As much as I desired this little one, oh how the Father desired me. I sang out in my tearful mess, and his love became real for me; his voice became more steadfast, and he spoke into my heart the revelation that *I was a kiss of the Father's love.* I became beautifully undone; the knot began unraveling as his words of truth sank deeper into my heart. The words I spoke over my son in the womb also expressed the Father's desire for me. Entering into the loss of my son felt like dying a million little deaths, but it was God's invitation to me to realize my true identity.

Two years later, Lance and I conceived our third son. I was completely in love without even seeing his face, because he was a gift of the Father's love to us. The sheer joy of being pregnant filled us with hopeful excitement. We were devastated when this pregnancy also ended in miscarriage.

Bafflingly, just a few short months later, we were informed that I was suffering from a serious kidney disease that made it extremely dangerous for me to be pregnant. We were hit with the reality that not only would we never have more biological children but also I wouldn't survive another pregnancy. I would lose my life and the life of a baby. It was a mind-numbing moment! My heart sank as my eyes met Lance's. Our mutual heartache was communicated in the silence of our tears.

How could I reconcile this news with the reality that my body is created to receive and cocreate new life? Every fiber of my being seemed to cry out, "I'm made to be a bearer of life, I am made for motherhood!" All our hope for children died. Reeling from the finality of this moment, I heard the words spoken by our friend a few years ago echo inside me, "You can have as many children as you want." Utterly bewildered, I felt an alarming question rise up within me: "Was that really God? How can that be true now?"

A few days later, a postcard from a friend arrived at just the right moment. I came completely undone as I read a beautiful quote from St. Francis de Sales, reminding me that God knows the crosses he gives to each of us—each one is a gift of his mercy.[1] Tears filled my eyes, and I knew in my devastation that this cross was the Father's crazy invitation into something more. Here he was, standing in the middle of what felt so messy, tenderly calling me into freedom and deeper love by drawing me into trust and into what it means to not be abandoned. I was encouraged to remain open and receptive before him and to give him my yes and permission to be loved. There was nowhere else to turn but into him. This became a moment of grace to respond with courage and vulnerability and trust in the truth that I am not abandoned in my suffering.

As I embraced my weakness, I experienced the strength of Jesus, his tender love, and his care. From some place inside myself I knew that the resurrection of my heart and my desires for family life would come and that I would bear life in ways unknown to me.

It is amazing how God placed just the right people in my life at just the right moments, often when I didn't realize that I needed them most. Lance and I met Bishop Sam at a youth conference, where he shared how his fatherhood is fully alive as he wrapped his arms around a spiritual son to his left and a spiritual daughter to his right. As we listened, Lance and I both felt a longing in our hearts for a spiritual father. With a boldness for which I will be forever grateful, Lance went up to Bishop Sam and simply asked him, "Would you be my spiritual father?" As Bishop Sam embraced us both, a beautiful lifelong relationship began to unfold. He has accompanied us with unconditional love, understanding, wisdom, and accountability.

God gave another beautiful gift to my heart that longed so deeply for family, as he soon brought Jim and Lois into our lives. They are an amazing married couple who are sages of love. Within their home I feel the deep history of love—it's written in the walls; I can feel it seep into my very bones. They have shared in the joys, the laughter, and the sorrowful tears of our lives. I didn't realize at first the legacy that Jim and Lois were leaving to us. The spiritual inheritance that has been passed on through the gift of their vast love has had a deep impact on our lives. We didn't have a word at that time for what they were, yet they were becoming spiritual parents to us. Their legacy of love has helped us in turn to pass on this inheritance to our own spiritual children.

An inheritance it was! It was only looking back that I realized how the Holy Spirit had been nurturing multiple children within our home for a long time. The seeds were planted through our commitment to relational youth ministry. We simply opened our doors to youth we were walking with. Relationships grew as the fruit of our genuine love, and became a part of our family life.

It began with Benjamin, who affectionately will say he is our *firstborn*, and Beth, who became a daily presence in our home for dinner, games, prayer, and conversations about life and Jesus. As Beth graduated from high school, she brought our relationship to college with her, and this naturally progressed into doing relational ministry with college students. This ministry, in turn, led to several more young adults asking us to be their spiritual parents.

I remember standing in my kitchen one day and reflecting on the reality of what God was birthing through our suffering. The fragrant aroma of family love came to my mind. This revelation burst open joy in my heart as the Lord began to show me how he planned all along to bring the gift of spiritual children into our lives. All of a sudden, the words spoken to us in prayer so many years ago came dancing through my heart: "You can have as many children as you want, and they just keep coming." I saw how this prayer was truly being fulfilled. I distinctly understood in that moment that God had intimately called us to spiritual parenthood.

Five years later, I witnessed my first spiritual son's ordination. Sitting in the pew the morning of Fr. Ben's thanksgiving Mass, I realized clearly in my heart that this moment was the fruit of our suffering. I remember tears streaming down my face and Jesus asking me, "Would you be willing to do it all over again?" With total shock and joy, I knew the answer without hesitation. It erupted and rose up within me: *Yes, yes! I would do it all over again. I would suffer all the losses again. It was worth this moment.*

God is creative, and he will not be outdone in his generosity. He is all about creating family. The fruit of our love is over thirty spiritual children. Some have become priests or religious, and others are married with children of their own. What we have experienced with our spiritual children is far more than just mentorship or spiritual companionship. It is living an *extra*ordinary life of love together.

# Take a Moment

1.  Pray with the following quotation from St. Francis de Sales:

    > The everlasting God has in his wisdom foreseen from
    > eternity the cross that he now presents to you as a gift
    > from his inmost Heart. This cross he now sends you
    > he has considered with his all-knowing eyes, under-
    > stood with his divine mind, tested with his wise justice,
    > warmed with loving arms and weighed with his own
    > hands to see that it be not one inch too large and not
    > one ounce too heavy for you. He has blessed it with his
    > Holy Name, anointed it with his consolation, taken one
    > last glance at you and your courage, and then sent it to
    > you from heaven, a special greeting from God to you,
    > an alms of the All-Merciful Love of God.

    a.  Read the quotation once and become familiar with the text.
    b.  Slowly read the quotation a second time.
    c.  Very, very slowly read the quotation a third time, paying
        attention to the words and phrases that rest in your heart.
        What is God speaking to you through this quotation?

2.  What crosses have you carried in your motherhood or desire
    to be a mother?

3.  Are you able to receive those crosses? Why or why not?

4.  Ask the Holy Spirit to reveal any hidden mercy in the cross you
    carry.

# It Is Never Too Late

## DEBRA HERBECK

This will not be one of those stories that I can tie up neatly with a beautiful ribbon. It's also not a step-by-step account of how I received inner healing and freedom. My life is not a finished or perfected product, and I am still in process, as I probably will be for a while. I have regrets—not that I am weak and broken but that it took me so long to pursue healing. I frankly never thought it was possible or that I deserved it, but I believe I am finally on the path to freedom and wholeness. Only you and God hold the road map to your own healing, but I pray my story fills you with the courage to begin or continue your journey.

Forty years ago. It was spring break my freshman year of college, and I sat on the front steps outside my parents' suburban home and set a match to the discharge paper from the abortion clinic. As I watched it go up in flames and the ashes settled at my feet, I thought, *No one needs to know about this. It's over now, and I can just get on with my life.* I hadn't painstakingly deliberated my decision or even considered the moral ramifications. Pregnancy was an inconvenience, and having a baby would interrupt my education and bring embarrassment to my family. Alone and afraid, I saw only one choice before me. I made the phone calls and scraped together the money, I walked to the clinic on a cold, snowy day, and I shut out my boyfriend and anyone else who might have helped me. This was my mess, and I would clean it up. This voice of shame and condemnation would keep me locked in a pattern of self-reliance and loneliness for years, unable to admit weakness or ask for help. Weeks later, as my body healed, I pushed away the memory of the abortion. But as the years passed, I realized that burning the evidence would not eradicate the effects of my choice, or the childhood wounds that had led me to that horrible day.

A few months later, I began an earnest-yet-cautious search for truth and meaning. My religious upbringing included a strong Jewish cultural identity and education. Everyone I knew was Jewish, and my exposure to Jesus and Christianity was almost nonexistent. As a secular Jew, I wasn't convinced that God existed, but if he did, he certainly wasn't personal or relevant to my daily life.

I grew up in a family that appeared to be a paragon of success—a nice home, material possessions, fun vacations, and prestige within the Jewish community. But even as a young child I sensed my mother's unhappiness, overheard her late-night drunken rants, and experienced her emotional distance. At times I wondered what I had done to make her love me less and what I could do to make her love me more. One day when I was ten years old, my siblings and I returned from school to find my mother in her car locked in the garage, threatening to end her life. My father came home from work, coaxed her out of the garage, handed her a double scotch on the rocks, and put her to bed. I was old enough to understand *what* was happening, I just didn't understand *why*. In a rare moment of transparency, my father explained to us three oldest kids that our mom's unhappiness stemmed from her never knowing her father, who had abandoned her at a young age. He ended the conversation with this definitive statement: "Your mom doesn't want help. We will never talk about this day again."

I didn't realize until years later that his comment had impressed into me our family protocol for handling difficult feelings or circumstances. I learned to suppress my negative emotions until even the expression of positive feelings such as joy, excitement, and enthusiasm became inaccessible and foreign to me. Over the course of my young childhood I experienced the trauma of repeated sexual molestation by an older relative, and then in early adolescence by a neighborhood boy. I kept these dark secrets that I thought would destroy my fragile family, and I believed an inner voice that told me it was somehow my fault. Even now as I write these words, I see that I've used one pithy sentence to describe immensely painful events in my young life. The ability to minimize hard things, tackle life on my own, and stifle my emotions became my unconscious coping mechanism.

By my sophomore year of high school, I had chosen to ignore my emotional life and our family dysfunction, and I put all my energy toward succeeding in academics, athletics, and popularity. Perhaps this would earn me the love and acceptance I so desperately desired. Halfway through that year, the illusion of my self-constructed "together" life was shattered when my older brother Mark, a freshman in college, was killed almost instantly in a violent car crash on his way home from school. Angry and confused, I had no help in processing my grief or making sense of the suffering, and a powerful fear of death settled over me. During the week, I studied intensely so I could get into a good university, and on the weekends, I turned to partying, drinking, music, and promiscuity to dull my pain.

My first roommate at the University of Michigan was also the first Christian I ever knew. Through her example and a close friendship with another authentic believer, I began to learn about Jesus. After nine months of seeking—reading the scriptures, counting the cost, and experiencing some divinely inspired dreams and visions—I was ready to welcome Jesus into my life as my Lord and Messiah. So many things about my life changed for the better as Jesus began to occupy first place. Despite my family's disapproval and distance, I grew in faith and confidence, and the fear of death no longer had a hold on me. I exercised leadership gifts and helped others come to know the Lord. I met my future husband and joined the Catholic Church. I brought my past sins into the light of the confessional, but in fear and shame I hid the deepest, darkest parts of my past from myself, others, and even God. I worked hard for God and served others, but allowing people to get too close felt risky. I never consciously rejected intimacy; in fact, I longed for it. I just never knew how to pursue or receive it. Instead, I stayed busy and focused on my present life—on ministry and my responsibilities to our growing family.

Over the years, often at my husband's prompting, I reluctantly sought out healing prayer, tried counseling sessions, inquired about possible retreats, and read some books, but in my mind, the thought of getting help was both terrifying and disheartening. So mostly I was resigned to limp along, dragging my wounds, my self-reliance, and my loneliness into my marriage, family life, and friendships. I taught and preached to other women about their value and dignity, but in the deepest, most wounded parts of me, I couldn't believe that I was worthy of love and intimacy, and that I was made to soar and not just survive.

In November of 2016, I was preparing to give a talk at a retreat for high school seniors titled "Obstacles to God's Friendship." With thirty years of youth ministry under my belt, I knew I had my talking points down. About an hour before I spoke, I clearly sensed God saying, "I want you to tell them specifically about your sinful, broken past and where those choices have led you. I want them to understand that *nothing* they have done can keep me from loving them." I balked at the thought of sharing my past with these students. Would they still respect me? Would they think I was a hypocrite? The most frightening thought emerged: Would they see me as I often viewed myself—broken, unlovable, and unforgivable? By God's grace, my love for these students and my desire to obey him helped me overcome my fears. I was able to tell them about the "unforgivable sin" I had kept hidden for almost forty years. Choking out the words, I forced myself to look directly at each of the young women I had mentored. In their expressions I saw surprise, but also compassion and love. As I finished my talk, the entire room stood in unison and applauded, and all seventy students lined up to personally hug and affirm me. That night, as the Year of Mercy in the Church drew to a close, I knew I was on the brink of allowing God's healing mercy to reach deep down and transform my pain. But was it too little, too late for me?

As I began to share the story of my abortion with others— my young adult children, family, friends, and acquaintances—I experienced both the terror of vulnerability and the relief of no longer carrying this heavy burden alone. Revealing the secret of my abortion and talking more freely about it as something I did, and not what defines me, were important hurdles. But as I began the painful process of pulling on that one now-visible thread, I realized that this tight knot can only be loosened, and true freedom can only come, as I allow the deeper pain of my childhood to be unveiled and healed.

Even as I write my story, fear and the pain of wounds threaten to silence my voice. I pray for the courage to speak and to continue my healing process not just for myself but for those who have no voice and never had a choice, including my own aborted child. And for all those who have suffered from my brokenness—my husband and family most of all—I pray that my long-overdue healing process will help me love them better and witness to the unfailing mercy of God for everyone. To all the women in hiding, afraid to bring their wounds into the light of God's mercy: Don't wait another minute, and certainly not almost a lifetime to seek wholeness and healing. Like me, you are worth so much more.

# Take a Moment

1. Pray with the following scripture passage from Ephesians 5:13–14:

   > But everything exposed by the light becomes visible, for everything that becomes visible is light.

   a. Read the scripture passage once and become familiar with the text.
   b. Slowly read the passage a second time.
   c. Very, very slowly read the passage a third time, paying attention to the words and phrases that rest in your heart. What is God speaking to you through this passage?

2. Are there parts of your story that you have chosen not to share with anyone else? If so, what prevents you from sharing?

3. How has your identity as mother been affected by the parts of your story that have not yet become visible in the light?

# The Narrow Road

## BARBRA CRUMPACKER

God can turn even our biggest mistakes into miracles. Praise the Lord. Because I have made mistakes in my life. For years, I condemned myself. My own worst enemy, I wallowed in the shame of my sin and regret—that is, until the unfailing truth and mercy of God penetrated the steely wall around my aching heart. After confiding in a wise and holy friend the painful secret that I did not feel worthy or deserving of forgiveness, he quickly countered, "Of course you don't. None of us do. That is why Jesus died for us." The truth he boldly spoke loosed the chain of regret that had kept me bound for decades. That truth led me from the lonely wide road of shame and regret that I had traveled for way too long to a path full of life and joy instead. This is how it unfolded.

I met my husband on the third day of college. It was love at first sight. I was not looking for a relationship on the third day of college, but there he was—bright, blue-eyed, handsome, and making my heart flip-flop. We started a courtship, and five years later we were married. While we had a very close relationship, it was not without difficulties. We both bore within our hearts our own share of childhood knots. Still, I knew, without a doubt, he was *the one*. As we

grew in our marriage, we could talk about almost everything. It was
what we *did not* discuss that eventually threatened to tear us apart.

During our first few years of marriage, as we were coping with
three small children and living on very little sleep, I discovered that
I had a chronic and debilitating illness. My hardworking husband,
who was under great stress trying to balance major job responsibilities, exhaustedly tried to manage the growing demands of our family life. While I felt blessed after the birth of our third child finally
to be able to stay home with the kids, it was quite an adjustment
after a thriving career. Our middle son (who we didn't know at the
time had ADHD) didn't seem to require much sleep. I survived on
only a couple of hours of good rest each night for more than two
years. A worsening flare of ulcerative colitis caused me to split my
time between the bathroom and the changing table with our two
babies. I was very sick and completely drained. While my children
were the joy of my life, having three little ones—two in diapers and
one that thought sleep was overrated—was truly exhausting. Our
life felt unmanageable.

Jon and I had dreamed of having a big family. I came from a
family of five, and we both loved the idea of a bustling house filled
with the joy of many pattering feet. Drowning in fear and self-reliance in that draining season, we chose mutually to close the door
permanently to that dream. We had used hormonal birth control
early in our relationship and quickly discovered the harsh effects on
my body. We decided that we could not put my tired body through
another pregnancy or return to birth control. It was just too much,
I was too sick, and both options seemed reckless. We reasoned
that a vasectomy seemed the most justified and responsible choice
available.

The decision was made. I did not seek counsel. I did not
attempt to understand the reasoning behind it. I did not consult
my doctors or my priest. All I knew was *the world* was all for it, and
everyone we knew affirmed our decision. The cure for my illness,

my exhaustion, my lack of freedom to give myself to my husband, would be a few snips of the surgical scissors.

On the day of the vasectomy, I made my way back to the operating room to be with my husband during the procedure. The moment I sat down next to him, I felt inexplicably unsettled. Everything in me wanted to run, dragging my sedated husband with me. I hoped the procedure would be over quickly so we could leave and I could shake this invasive sense of dread. As the doctor and staff filed into the room, their conversations made me feel embarrassed and insignificant. The atmosphere was filled with superficial laughter and crude remarks. Suddenly this *minor* procedure no longer seemed so minor. A panic welled up inside of me—*This is a big deal!* Did they understand what they were taking away with those scissors? In that moment, I realized that we had taken this decision *way* too lightly. The echo of shame and regret afterward was deafening. *We had asked for this. We had chosen this path. We made an irrevocable mistake.*

We went back to our everyday normal life, hoping at least to rekindle the intimacy and freedom we longed for. Instead, we felt anything but normal. Our intimate relationship suffered. It continued to suffer until we reached a crisis point—a crisis that most marriages do not survive. We desperately needed help!

The truth is that God had never been invited into our bedroom. We didn't think he belonged there. The bedroom was certainly not meant to be a spiritual place. I knew babies were from God and an incredible gift, but not the way they *got here*—that was a different story. It had never, *ever* dawned on me that sexual intimacy was a sacred gift from God. That just seemed ridiculous . . . or was it?

We were introduced to a book by Christopher West on the teachings of St. John Paul II. Called *Good News about Sex and Marriage*, this book did not initially thrill my husband. Reading it, however, blew both of us away.

Over time, our paradigm on sex and marriage began to shift. God placed very holy people in our path, understanding souls who were patient with us and gave us the opportunity to uncover a completely new world. A world that had been hidden from us—or, more aptly put, one we had hidden from. As we studied the revelations of St. John Paul II, it all began to make sense. God created us with the capacity to create life. The Church's teaching on sexuality and childbearing did not consist of arbitrary rules but instead offered borders to protect our greater freedom. We thought contraception and sterilization would give us freedom, but in fact, they destroy freedom in relationship. As these hidden truths came into focus, we desperately wished we had known these realities sooner. If we had known, maybe we wouldn't have made so many mistakes. Maybe we would have been spared some of the pain and suffering. Maybe we would have lived in greater joy and freedom. The regret consumed me. My husband's perspective was different; he would gently remind me that God is bigger than our mistakes and can turn them into good.

The truth is, God *can*. Sometime after receiving this new revelation, and the gift of truth spoken from my wise friend in regard to my regret, we made a decision that seemed absurd to most of our family and friends. We decided to attend a natural family planning (NFP) class. A sterilized couple in a fertility class is a bit like a vegetarian at a meat market. We seemed out of place. We had no clue why we felt called to attend, but that is where we found ourselves. We wondered if maybe the call was to follow our natural cycles of fertility as if we hadn't had the procedure, or maybe to be aware enough of our fertility to teach our own kids. Whatever the reason, NFP was enlightening. Still, I couldn't help but dwell on the fact that it was too late. We had bucked God's will and made our choice. But as usual, God had more for us to learn. He was patiently planting seeds along this narrow path that were taking root as we followed his lead. He walked with us as we continued to study, pray, and talk. Then one day, it all became clear. With deep conviction, we felt called to undergo a vasectomy reversal. I was still too scared to have another baby due to my illness, so there was no intention on my part to have another child. My better half, on the other hand, was always open to more pattering feet around the house. Ultimately, we felt that we were supposed to take this next step in order to experience God's true freedom and peace.

We were led to a doctor in Texas who specialized in vasectomy reversals. He considered it his ministry. The contrast between the vasectomy and the reversal procedure was stark. The doctor embraced us as soon as we crossed the threshold. He sat us down and began showing us the baby pictures plastered all over the walls, explaining brightly that each one was born after a reversal. Mincing no words, I explained that we weren't there to have another baby, only to get right with God. After all, God only asked us to do the reversal; he didn't mention anything about *more babies*. I knew we had NFP in our toolbox. The doctor just smiled.

The procedure began with prayer. The doctor played Christian music and talked to us about our family, our dreams, and our goals. The atmosphere was so respectful, so peaceful, so loving, and it felt as though Jesus and Mary were on either side of us. *This* was the right decision.

With this new and fertile ground and God's patiently planted seeds, our dream of having more children began to sprout. The reversal process itself was emotionally and physically healing for both of us. The flare of colitis that had previously seemed unrelenting abated. With a *yes* only a month after the reversal, we were blessed to conceive our fourth child. A beautiful baby boy was born twelve years after our first. Each time we watch our son walk onto the baseball field, laugh at the dinner table, or kiss us good night, we shudder to think what we almost missed.

We were duped by this world. I am not proud of that. Thankfully, our eyes were opened to the perfectly laid path for our sexuality that had been in front of us the whole time. Even though our shame and regret shrouded it from view, God never stopped pointing the way. He does want to be a part of our lives—our *entire* lives. God's truth requires us to trust him, and that trust leads to freedom, and that freedom leads to joy, and that joy leads to fulfillment. The narrow path leads to life (Mt 7:14).

# Take a Moment

1. Pray with the following scripture from Matthew 7:13–14:

   > Enter through the narrow gate; for the gate is wide and the road broad that leads to destruction, and those who enter through it are many. How narrow the gate and constricted the road that leads to life. And those who find it are few.

   a. Read the scripture passage once and become familiar with the text.
   b. Slowly read the passage a second time.
   c. Very, very slowly read the passage a third time, paying attention to the words and phrases that rest in your heart. What is God speaking to you through this passage?
2. Is there an area in your life where you sense you are walking on the wrong track? Or in the wrong direction?
3. Would you be willing to stop and ask for direction? If so, ask the Holy Spirit to reveal to you what direction to walk for deeper freedom and to become more fully alive in him.

# This Is My Body

## CARRIE SCHUCHTS DAUNT

There was a time in my life when I thought being an underwear model was a legitimate career choice. Don't laugh! I am serious. Just because *you* can't imagine this five-foot, pasty white, ministry-loving mother of eight lounging around in skivvies doesn't mean it couldn't happen. Everyone knows that adolescence has a way of distorting reality. The only thing I thought I excelled at was looking good in a bikini. In my juvenile mind, this translated to only two known professional options: lifeguard or underwear model. I spent my summers lifeguarding and knew I couldn't make a living doing that forever, so underwear model won by default.

Shallow, vain, and ridiculous, I know. It's not like I was born with this distorted view. In fact, I grew up with the security and love of both my parents. Although they were college students when they married, they juggled the demands of school, work, and parenthood well. My little sister (who was born only a couple short years after me) and I both knew we were loved. My parents tell me I was a confident and happy little girl who loved to talk. Family legend has it I spoke unusually early, in full sentences before I celebrated my first birthday.

However, even with the arsenal of words I mastered at a young age, somehow I could not verbalize the terror I felt being left at school. From the moment I walked into my kindergarten classroom, I realized I was very different from my peers. While I loved people, I was a sensitive child and I struggled to fit in. School was a challenge for me both academically and socially. I would spend hours in the classroom and on the playground confused and isolated. It wasn't until third grade that I was finally diagnosed with a learning disability. Although my parents and the school worked hard to remediate my delays, I spent the rest of my elementary and middle school years playing catch-up.

My middle school years in particular were humiliating. My peers, even those I believed were my friends, constantly ridiculed me. A gang of neighborhood boys was particularly cruel on the bus rides into school. There wasn't a day that went by that my tormentors didn't remind me of my many imperfections. I wore braces because of an overbite, and they called me "Bucky"; I had kinky and unruly curly hair before the advent of the flat iron and was called "Poodle"; I had an outbreak of adolescent warts on my fingers and was nastily christened "Toad." Their jeers and taunts caused so much shame and misery that I would call home "sick" at least once a week, begging my parents to pick me up. I hated school. I hated my classmates. Most of all, I hated myself. By the time I reached high school, my self-esteem was abysmally low. I wanted so desperately to fit in and be accepted that I grasped at any opportunity that came my way.

During my sophomore year in high school, the opportunity came. After joining the swim team, I started to enjoy some unfamiliar attention. Boys that had once avoided me were now going out of their way to speak to me. This newfound interest had little to do with who I was or how well I swam. It had everything to do with how well I filled out a swimsuit. I relished the new acceptance of my peers. The attention felt redemptive; I was like the ugly duckling that became the beautiful-breasted swan. However, instead of swimming quietly away like the humble fowl in the story, I fluffed my feathers and strutted ridiculously in front of the other gawking ducks. To cover my deep insecurity and fear of isolation, I grasped at the attention I was receiving, many times putting myself in situations and places that created an even deeper shame.

By the grace of God, I met the right person in the wrong place. Over spring break at the beach, I met a boy who was brilliant, confident, and had a real plan for his life. He had just accepted a congressional appointment to the United States Air Force Academy and in a few short months was moving to Colorado. We dated casually, knowing long-distance relationships never last, and stunned ourselves by staying together all through college.

The winter of my senior year in college, I was surprised by a romantic marriage proposal and news that my fiancé had been secretly taking classes to become confirmed in my Catholic faith. We were married a few short months after graduation in my home parish. Everything about the day had been perfectly planned— except for one small detail. The church was under construction but was scheduled to be finished earlier that summer. Only weeks before the wedding, our beloved pastor called to let us know that the church would not be ready for our big day. Graciously he offered us a few options. We could call around and see if there was another church nearby open on that date (there wasn't), change the date (invitations had already gone out), or ignore the orange mesh, cones, and general construction hazards that littered the grounds and walk down the aisle anyway. Reluctantly we chose the latter. Despite the mess, the ceremony was beautiful.

After the wedding, my father shared a few words. I can't remember every heartfelt thing he spoke, but I distinctly recall him drawing an analogy between the construction zone and real life. *Nothing is always perfect or pretty; often, real beauty comes with the mess of restoration.* As a seasoned Christ-centered family therapist, he was well aware of the messiness that marks real life.

He also knew that tearing down the old framework would make way for something new and beautiful.

A few short years later, we found ourselves right in the center of our first construction zone. We were quickly blessed with three wonderful children. When we found out we were having our third child, my self-sacrificing husband gave up his promising military career so we could move closer to our family. While the move was a blessing on many levels, returning home unexpectedly stirred up places in my heart that I had managed to ignore while living in another state under a new name. As I tried to find my place with friends and family, I felt an old and uneasy awkwardness I had conveniently forgotten.

One acquaintance in particular stirred this feeling of inadequacy with precision. She was one of the few moms that I knew in town, and she willingly included me in her activities. Although she was inclusive, she seemed to gain pleasure from exposing my weakness. One day, I foolishly shared one of my deepest insecurities with her only to have her make a distasteful joke about it minutes later. I heard a familiar voice echoing in my head: *See, nobody really likes you.* I desperately wanted to make this voice go away. But the harder I tried, the louder it screamed. *Don't even try to make friends; nobody will ever really want to be your friend. You don't belong.*

My heart was transported back to middle school. The taunting, unkind words that were spoken over my sensitive little-girl heart all those years ago were being thrown at me all over again by the screaming voice in my head. *Get away from me. Nobody wants you around.* In this season, many of my hidden childhood lies were unleashed.

After giving birth to three children, I no longer had my perfect figure to hide behind. While I had always dreamed of a big family and deeply loved being a wife and mother, I never knew the toll that childbirth and childbearing would take on my body. For years, I had hidden my insecurities behind the pride that even if the rest of me was a mess, I still could turn heads and invoke the admiration of envy. Not anymore. No one even noticed me. Similar to the church on my wedding day, I was presented with an ugly reality that I had to somehow learn to embrace.

During this painful period, I was drawn to another young mother at my parish. From her peaceful demeanor and gentle spirit, I assumed she had it all together. One day she vulnerably shared her own struggles and battle with shame. Hearing her acknowledge the places in her heart that were broken struck me with a heartening knowledge that I was not alone in my shame. She was feeling the same need to hide. Instead of hiding, however, she was bringing these dark, shrouded places into the light. My response to her vulnerability was a deep admiration. I was drawn to her. She was someone I could actually trust with my heart. I wanted to live in the kind of freedom and transparency that she modeled.

Having been allowed to enter her messiest places, I finally began to acknowledge my own cobwebbed, covered spaces. Behind the shame was the little girl crying out for acceptance. I prayed that God would give me the courage to face my pain as bravely as my new friend had, and come out on the other side with greater wholeness and freedom.

In his providence, God answered my prayers with another positive pregnancy test. The fourth child in five years. Didn't we know where babies come from? Many people, even in my own family, thought we were being irresponsible. Before we were married, we gave our yes to God to follow the Church's teaching on natural child spacing and openness to life, but this felt like too much too fast. To say we felt overwhelmed was a gross understatement. We already felt stretched beyond our limits. My husband worked many hours a week with the grind of professional life, and we both dabbled in ministry projects on the side. If that wasn't enough, we were in the process of building a new home that was taking longer than expected. Our current house sold much quicker than we predicted, so my parents graciously opened their home to us until our new house was complete.

Toward the end of my pregnancy, I was struggling to get around. I seemed to be expanding at a quicker rate then I did with the other children. Everywhere I went, people would gape at my enormous belly, often asking if I was expecting twins. As people gawked at my swollen middle, the whisper of shame was relentless. *Why am I so repulsive?*

One day early in this pregnancy, I found a rare moment alone in eucharistic adoration. As soon as I sat in the Lord's presence, a vivid picture flashed through my mind. It was a picture of a large pair of granny panties. The ugliest, biggest, and most unflattering pair imaginable. After laughing aloud in the quiet chapel, I asked, *Lord, what does that mean*? Almost audibly, I heard, *You will be stretched.* God was speaking, and I was trying to listen. A week before I gave birth, he spoke again through a friend who received in prayer that *this baby will be a gift of God's mercy.*

Six weeks before the new house was complete, I gave birth to a beautiful baby boy who weighed nearly ten pounds. Exhausted, I nursed our baby on the bed as my husband sat at my feet, poring over lists of boys' names. Every time he offered a name, I would ask the meaning and shrug off each suggestion. Finally he asked, "Carrie, what about *John*?"

"What does it mean?" I sighed, dreading another couple of hours of this back-and-forth.

"God's merciful love," he answered without hesitation.

I was immediately reminded of the word my friend spoke about this baby being a *gift of mercy*. "That's it!" I cried, nearly jumping out of the bed with a flailing baby in my arms. "John David. After God's beloved in the Old and the New Testaments."

"We can call him Jack for short," my husband inserted.

Jack was much more demanding than my other babies. He was temperamental and constantly hungry. He would scream until he latched on to eat and would stay latched for hours at a time, hungrily nursing on my torn and often infected breasts. The whole pregnancy and delivery had already taken quite a toll on my tired body. My body, my house, and my capacity to handle the many demands of my growing family had exhausted every part of me. I remember thinking, *God, there is nothing left of me to give . . .*

Then one miraculous night during a marathon nursing session, in our newly completed home, Baby Jack looked up at me with his dazzling blue eyes and smiled the most precious smile. The love! I was nearly bursting with bliss. Every bit of my selfish vanity disappeared in his utterly dependent and adoring gaze. I had been stretched and taut and drained for this precise moment of mercy. My eyes welled up with tears of immense gratitude. Glancing down at this delicate life in my arms, I uttered the words that astonished and transformed me: "This is my body, which will be given for you" (Lk 22:19).

After that day, I was different. I expanded with a greater capacity. Shame no longer drained me. I was filled with the deep, rich fruit of love. A love that was born from love, which no longer took the form of lustful attraction or fleeting feelings but of sacrifice and self-gift.

Thirteen years and four more kids later, my life is full and beautiful. I am proud to say that everywhere I go people notice me. Driving a shockingly chic, big, blue passenger van, I am hard to miss. Even though I spent most of my life battling lies about my self-worth and belonging, I now know—I am enough. *I am more than enough.* My feminine frame covers my most captivating capacity to cultivate life. I spent all those years searching for the perfect profession, and I can now confidently say I have found it. Motherhood.

## Take a Moment

1.   Pray with the following scripture passage from Romans 12:1–2:

> I urge you therefore, brothers, by the mercies of God, to
> offer your bodies as a living sacrifice, holy and pleasing
> to God, your spiritual worship. Do not conform your-
> selves to this age but be transformed by the renewal of
> your mind, that you may discern what is the will of God,
> what is good and pleasing and perfect.

   a.  Read the scripture passage once and become familiar with
      the text.

   b.  Slowly read the passage a second time.

   c.  Very, very slowly read the passage a third time, paying
      attention to the words and phrases that rest in your heart.
      What is God speaking to you through this passage?

2. What does *offering your bodies as a living sacrifice* look like in
   your motherhood?

3. In what ways do you *conform to this age* in your vocation?

4. In prayer, ask the Holy Spirit to lead you to God's *perfect and
   pleasing* will.

# Inner Healing Prayer

## MOTHER IDENTITY

## BOB SCHUCHTS

As you engage in this meditative and contemplative prayer experience, allow the Holy Spirit to lead you. Pause after each step to record your experiences in a journal.

1.  Ask the Holy Spirit to show you the specific and general ways you have found fulfillment in your role as a mother—biological, adoptive, or spiritual.
2.  Ask the Holy Spirit to reveal to you how and when you were wounded in your identity as mother.
3.  Ask the Holy Spirit to reveal to you the knots that have kept your heart from living freely as a mother. What are the lies underlying these knots?
4.  Ask the Holy Spirit to allow you to experience life in the Holy Family. Can you imagine what it would be like to have Jesus as a son, loving, honoring, and obeying you, and Joseph as a

husband, coparenting with you with love and respect? Write in your prayer journal what you saw, thought, felt, and desired.

5.   Ask the Holy Spirit to reveal to you the truth about your identity as mother in any areas where the lies took root in your heart. Record these truths in your journal.

6.   Finally, ask Mary, the Blessed Mother, to untie the knots that were formed in your relationship with your children (or spouse as coparent).

7.   Close with a prayer of thanksgiving to Mary and Jesus for teaching you how to be the mother you desire to be.

# APPENDIX I

# Wounds, Beliefs, and Vows

Throughout this book, *wounds, beliefs* (lies and judgments), and *inner vows* are referenced. Wounds refer to the trauma we experience in our lives. Beliefs in this context refer to our negative belief system about others and ourselves. There are two types of beliefs: lies and judgments. A lie is what we believe about ourselves that is contrary to our true identity. A judgment is what we believe about someone else, typically in relation to a hurt or trauma that distorts their true identity. Inner vows are agreements we make with these beliefs that keep us bound in a fortress of self-protection.[1]

Included in this appendix are specific prayers developed by the John Paul II Healing Center to combat our fortresses of unhealthy self-protection.[2]

# PRAYER FOR RENOUNCING INNER VOWS

Father, I acknowledge that I have tried to save myself rather than rely on you for my salvation. Please forgive me for my sins of pride and self-sufficiency. I acknowledge that my effort to protect myself has left me imprisoned behind walls that keep me from freely giving and receiving love. I desire to be free of this bondage that has come as a result of my own choices. In the name of Jesus, I renounce the inner vow that _____ (details of that vow). I ask you to release me from the bondage of this vow now. Thank you. Amen.

# PRAYER FOR RENOUNCING IDENTITY LIES

In the name of Jesus Christ, I renounce the lie that _____ ("I am alone," "I am ugly," "Nothing will ever change," "I am not loved," "If I trust I will die," etc.). And in Jesus' name, and through the Holy Spirit, I ask you, Father, to reveal the truth of my identity where these identity lies have taken hold of my heart. Amen.

# PRAYER FOR RENOUNCING JUDGMENT[3]

Father, I acknowledge that I have judged _____ (name). I realize that I did this to protect myself from feelings of vulnerability and powerlessness in order not to be hurt. I also realize this judgment is sin and keeps me bound. I ask now for forgiveness and for release of me and _____ (the person judged) from the bondage of this condemnation and isolation. In the name of Jesus, I renounce the judgment of _____ (name) that he/she is _____ (identify specific judgments). I know I cannot change my own heart without

your grace, so I ask you to give me your heart of compassion for
_____ (name). Amen.

# Our Lady Undoer of Knots Prayer

Dearest Holy Mother, Most Holy Mary, you undo the knots that suffocate your children. Extend your merciful hands to me. I entrust to you today this knot [mention your request here] and all the negative consequences that it provokes in my life.

Mary, Undoer of Knots, pray for me.

Virgin Mary, Mother of fair love, Mother who never refuses to come to the aid of a child in need, Mother whose hands never cease to serve your beloved children because they are moved by the divine love and immense mercy that exist in your heart, cast your compassionate eyes upon me and see the snarl of knots that exists in my life. You know very well how desperate I am, my pain, and how I am bound by these knots. Mary, Mother to whom God entrusted the undoing of the knots in the lives of his children, I entrust into your hands the ribbon of my life. No one, not even the evil one himself, can take it away from your precious care. In your hands there is no knot that cannot be undone. Powerful Mother, by

your grace and intercessory power with your Son and my Liberator,
Jesus, take into your hands today this knot.

[Mention your request here]

I beg you to undo it for the glory of God, once and for all. You
are my hope. O my Lady, you are the only consolation God gives
me, the fortification of my feeble strength, the enrichment of my
destitution, and, with Christ, the freedom from my chains. Hear my
plea. Keep me, guide me, protect me, O safe refuge! Mary, Undoer
of Knots, pray for me. Amen.[1]

# APPENDIX III

*Additional Resources*

**Counseling and Individual Healing**
Catholic Psychotherapy Association
www.catholicpsychotherapy.org
402-885-9272

**Post-Abortion Resources**
Rachel's Vineyard
www.rachelsvineyard.org
877-467-3463

**National Abortion Recovery**
www.internationalhelpline.org
866-482-5433

**Elizabeth Ministry**
www.elizabethministry.org
920-766-9380

**Miscarriage Resources**
Elizabeth Ministry
www.elizabethministry.org

**Catholic Miscarriage Support**
www.Catholicmiscarriagesupport.com

**Infertility Resources**
Saint Paul VI Institute
popepaulvi.com
402-390-6600

**Same-Sex Attraction**
Eden Invitation: Original Personhood beyond the
    LGBT+ Paradigm
www.edeninvitation.com

**Pornography and Sexual Addiction Recovery Resources**
Reclaim Sexual Health
www.ReclaimSexualHealth.com
920-766-9380

**Events, Retreats, and Conferences**
John Paul II Healing Center
www.jpiihealingcenter.org

**Theology of the Body Institute**
www.tobinstitute.org

**Bible Study Groups**
Walking with Purpose
www.walkingwithpurpose.com
844-492-5597

**Podcasts**
www.abidingtogetherpodcast.com

## NOT THAT GIRL

1. Stephen Schwartz, *Wicked: A New Musical: Original Broadway Cast Recording* (New York: Decca Broadway, 2003).

2. John Paul II Healing Center, Tallahassee, FL, jpiihealingcenter.org.

3. Theology of the Body Institute, Lima, PA, http://tobinstitute.org.

4. John Paul II, *Man and Woman He Created Them: A Theology of the Body*, trans. Michael M. Waldstein (Boston: Pauline Books and Media, 2006).

5. "Thérèse de Lisieux Quotes," Goodreads, accessed April 30, 2019, http://www.goodreads.com/author/quotes/248952.Th_r_se_de_Lisieux.

## DISCORD TO HARMONY

1. "Gordon," review of *Songs for Life,* by the Pierce Sisters, Amazon, accessed April 27, 2019, https://www.amazon.com/gp/aw/cr/B0002659GM/ref=mw_dp_cr.

2. *Frozen*, directed by Chris Buck and Jennifer Lee (Hollywood: Walt Disney Animation Studios, 2013).

3. "Ludwig van Beethoven Quotes," Goodreads, https://www.goodreads.com/quotes/501895-don-t-only-practice-your-art-but-force-your-way-into.

## RAVISH MY HEART

1. Christopher West, *Good News about Sex and Marriage: Answers to Your Honest Questions about Catholic Teaching* (Cincinnati, OH: Servant, 2018).

2. John Paul II, *Man and Woman He Created Them: A Theology of the Body*, trans. Michael Waldstein (Chicago: Pauline Books and Media, 2006).

## NEVER ALONE

1. "Danielle LaPorte Quotes," Goodreads, accessed April 30, 2019, http://www.goodreads.com/quotes/972995-can-you-remember-who-you-were-before-the-world-told.

2. "Augustine of Hippo Quotes," Goodreads, accessed April 30, 2019, http://www.goodreads.com/quotes/164594-in-my-deepest-wound-i-saw-your-glory-and-it.

## THE FULFILLMENT OF ALL DESIRE

1. John Paul II, *Man and Woman He Created Them.*

## LOVE RECLAIMED

1. Laurie Hall, *An Affair of the Mind: One Woman's Courageous Battle to Salvage Her Family from the Devastation of Pornography* (Wheaton, IL: Tyndale House, 2003).

## EXTRAORDINARY LOVE

1. "Francis de Sales Quotes," Goodreads, accessed April 30, 2019, http://www.goodreads.com/quotes/8054485-the-everlasting-god-has-in-his-wisdom-foreseen-from-eternity.

## APPENDIX I: WOUNDS, BELIEFS, AND VOWS

1. See Bob Schuchts, *Be Healed: A Guide to Encountering the Powerful Love of Jesus in Your Life* (Notre Dame, IN: Ave Maria Press, 2014), 113.

2. See Bob Schuchts, *Healing the Whole Person* (workbook and CDs available at www.jpiihealing.org).

3. *I AM Ministry Training* Workbook, 24, www.jpiihealingcenter.org.

## APPENDIX II: OUR LADY UNDOER OF KNOTS PRAYER

1. "Pray More Novenas," www.praymorenovenas.com/mary-undoer-knots-novena.

# Contributors

*Judy Bailey* is the executive director of the John Paul II Healing Center in Tallahassee, Florida. Judy has been married to her husband, Don, for more than thirty years and has two adult sons, Blake and Devon. Together, Judy and Don coauthored *She Called My Name*, which documents their miraculous conversion story and their introduction to the Catholic Church.

*Mary Bielski* has been involved in ministry for more than fifteen years, speaking to thousands of youth and young adults around the nation. Mary is passionate about drawing people to the beauty of the Catholic faith, a deeper love for Christ, the Eucharist, and the call to holiness. Mary has a bachelor's degree in theology and psychology and a master's degree in theological studies with a focus in pastoral leadership from Notre Dame Seminary in New Orleans, Louisiana.

*Lisa Brenninkmeyer* is the founder and chief purpose officer of Walking with Purpose, a Catholic women's Bible study program. Raised as an evangelical Protestant, she entered the Catholic Church in 1991. She has authored the book *Walking with Purpose: Seven Priorities that Make Life Work*, nine women's Bible studies, six young adult Bible studies, and a middle school girls' program.

*Kristen Blake* serves as a full-time member of the John Paul II Healing Center team. After experiencing a deep conversion through the Church's teaching on marriage and sexuality, Kristen desires to share it with others who are longing for freedom and healing. Kristen resides in Tallahassee with her husband, Stephen.

*Carolyn Pierce Brown* is passionate about music as an intersection of heaven and earth. She received her bachelor's degrees in philosophy and theology from Franciscan University and a master's degree in sacred music with a voice concentration from the Catholic University of America. Born in Philadelphia, she now lives in St. Augustine, Florida, with her five children and her husband, Luis.

*Danielle Chodorowski* is a life coach and speaker who is passionate about journeying with other women to be fully alive, standing in who they are created to be. Danielle is a wife to Dave and homeschooling mother of six amazing kids, who make their home in the beautiful countryside of Wisconsin.

*Barbra Crumpacker* is a graduate of Florida State University with a bachelor's degree in nutrition and fitness. Barbra works as an oncology dietitian, where she has served cancer patients for more than twenty years. Her greatest joy comes from spending time with her husband and their four children.

*Jeannie Hannemann* is the founder of Elizabeth Ministry International and Navigate Betrayal. She is also codirector of the program Reclaim Sexual Health. She is an internationally known speaker and author on topics related to sexuality, childbearing, and relationships, with a special focus on helping those struggling with, or affected by, sexual sins.

*Debra Herbeck* is a Messianic Jewish Catholic who has dedicated her life to helping young women know the personal love of Jesus Christ and walk in their dignity as daughters of God. Debbie is the founder and director of Pine Hills Girls' Camp and Be Love Revolution, as well as an author and speaker. Her greatest "accomplishment," however, is her marriage to Peter, their four young-adult children, and their seven grandchildren.

*Colleen Nixon* is Tallahassee, Florida's homegrown wildflower who has been singing since before she learned to speak. Colleen moved to Nashville and received her bachelor's degree from Belmont University in commercial voice. She has released five albums. When Colleen isn't singing, she is kept very busy caring for her four children. She is beyond grateful for her husband, Titus, who helps her share the gift of music with the world.

*Melissa Perez* is a contemplative, extravert, Catholic, homeschool mother of two, who married her high school sweetheart after meeting him again at their ten-year high school reunion. She and her husband have spent more than ten years serving as marriage coaches and mentors, as well as health-care advocates for patients with rare metabolic disorders. She is the event coordinator for the John Paul II Healing Center's Undone women's conference and loves seeing how God moves beautifully in people's hearts and lives.

*Nicole Rodríguez* is a collaborator and speaker for Undone: Freedom for the Feminine Heart at the John Paul II

Healing Center. She is a certified spiritual director, and has twenty years of experience speaking at young adult conferences. Nicole and her husband of twenty-three years, Lance, are parents to three biological sons who are now powerful intercessors in heaven and are blessed to share their hearts and lives with more than thirty spiritual children. Nicole has dedicated her life to bearing witness to the power of spiritual maternity; her passion is to reveal the splendor and strength of true vulnerability in which women's hearts are set free, transformed, and empowered by the endless love of God.

*Bob Schuchts* is the bestselling author of *Be Healed*, *Be Transformed*, and *Be Devoted* and the founder of the John Paul II Healing Center in Tallahassee, Florida.

*Jen Settle* became a Consecrated Virgin in 2017. She has worked for the Theology of the Body Institute in Philadelphia since 2008 and now serves as its director of programs. She teaches theology of the body throughout the country and has a deep love for intercessory prayer.

*Dorothy Derzypolski Wagner* has a bachelor's degree in philosophy from Florida State University and a master's degree in theology from Franciscan University. Dorothy is married to Nicholas Wagner. Throughout their marriage, they have served in overseas missions, teaching courses on the theology of the body, and most recently cofounded a hurricane relief mission called Mission850.com. Together they homeschool their four children and reside in Tallahassee, Florida.

*Carrie Schuchts Daunt* is a presenter and prayer minister for the John Paul II Healing Center in Tallahassee, Florida. She developed the material for the center's *Undone* women's event.

Daunt earned her bachelor's degree in speech communication from Berry College in Rome, Georgia. She teaches classes at home and for the Sacred Heart Home Educators cooperative, where she is also on the executive board. Daunt also has led women's bible studies and presented talks on marriage, Theology of the Body, and authentic femininity for her parish and diocese.

She lives with her husband, Duane, and their eight children in Tallahasee.

Facebook: CarrieDaunt
Twitter: @CarrieDaunt
Instagram: @CarrieDaunt


*Sr. Miriam James Heidland, S.O.L.T.*, is a Catholic speaker and podcaster. She is the author of *Loved As I Am*.

# Books by Bob Schuchts
## FOUNDER OF THE JOHN PAUL II HEALING CENTER

In the tradition of such beloved spiritual teachers as Francis MacNutt and Michael Scanlan, *Be Healed: A Guide to Encountering the Powerful Love of Jesus in Your Life* offers in book form Bob Schuchts's popular program for spiritual, emotional, and physical healing through the power of the Holy Spirit and the sacraments.

God has given us the perfect solution to transform our lives and grow spiritually in spite of our sinfulness—the sacraments. Based on more than thirty-five years of experience as a therapist and decades spent leading retreats, Bob Schuchts demonstrates how each of the seven sacraments is a life-changing encounter with Christ.

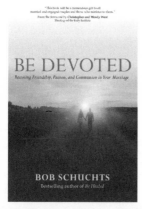

Based on his popular healing conferences, forty years of marriage, and decades of clinical work as a couple's therapist, Bob Schuchts presents his first resource for married couples. *Be Devoted* delivers sound Catholic teaching, rich storytelling, and practical tools for healing, along with psychological insights and expertise to help couples create a relationship that is rich in trust, passion, and unity.